General editor: Graham Handley MA PH D

Brodie's Notes on William Shakespeare's
Much Ado About Nothing

Graham Handley MA PH D
Formerly Principal Lecturer and Head of English Department, The College of All Saints, Tottenham

Pan Books London and Sydney

First published 1985 by Pan Books Ltd
Cavaye Place, London SW10 9PG
9 8 7 6 5 4 3 2 1
© Pan Books Ltd 1985
ISBN 0 330 50203 4
Photoset by Parker Typesetting Service, Leicester
Printed and bound in Great Britain by
Richard Clay (The Chaucer Press) Ltd, Bungay, Suffolk

Other titles by Graham Handley in the Brodie's Notes series:
As You Like It
Macbeth
Twelfth Night
The Winter's Tale

Contents

Line references in these Notes are to the
Arden Shakespeare: Much Ado About Nothing,
but as references are also given to particular acts
and scenes, the Notes may be used with any
edition of the play.

Preface

This student revision aid is based on the principle that in any close examination of Shakespeare's plays 'the text's the thing'. Seeing a performance, or listening to a tape or record of a performance, is essential and is in itself a valuable and stimulating experience in understanding and appreciation. However, a real evaluation of Shakespeare's greatness, of his universality and of the nature of his literary and dramatic art, can only be achieved by constant application to the texts of the plays themselves. These revised editions of Brodie's Notes are intended to supplement that process through detailed critical commentary.

The first aim of each book is to fix the whole play in the reader's mind by providing a concise summary of the plot, relating it back, where appropriate, to its source or sources. Subsequently the book provides a summary of each scene, followed by *critical comments*. These may convey its importance in the dramatic structure of the play, creation of atmosphere, indication of character development, significance of figurative language etc, and they will also explain or paraphrase difficult words or phrases and identify meaningful references. At the end of each act revision questions are set to test the student's specific and broad understanding and appreciation of the play.

An extended critical commentary follows this scene by scene analysis. This embraces such major elements as characterization, imagery, the use of blank verse and prose, soliloquies and other aspects of the play which the editor considers need close attention. The paramount aim is to send the reader back to the text. The book concludes with a series of revision questions which require a detailed knowledge of the play; the first of these has notes by the editor of what *might* be included in a written answer. The intention is to stimulate and to guide; the whole emphasis of this commentary is to encourage the student's *involvement* in the play, to develop disciplined critical responses and thus promote personal enrichment through the imaginative experience of our greatest writer.

Graham Handley

Shakespeare and the Elizabethan Playhouse

William Shakespeare was born in Stratford-upon-Avon in 1564, and there are reasons to suppose that he came from a relatively prosperous family. He was probably educated at Stratford Grammar School and, at the age of eighteen, married Anne Hathaway, who was twenty-six. They had three children, a girl born shortly after their marriage, followed by twins in 1585 (the boy died in 1596). It seems likely that Shakespeare left for London shortly after a company of visiting players had visited Stratford in 1585, for by 1592 – according to the jealous testimony of one of his fellow-writers Robert Greene – he was certainly making his way both as actor and dramatist. The theatres were closed because of the plague in 1593; when they reopened Shakespeare worked with the Lord Chamberlain's men, later the King's men, and became a shareholder in each of the two theatres with which he was most closely associated, the Globe and the Blackfriars. He later purchased New Place, a considerable property in his home town of Stratford, to which he retired in 1611; there he entertained his great contemporary Ben Jonson (1572–1637) and the poet Michael Drayton (1563–1631). An astute businessman, Shakespeare lived comfortably in the town until his death in 1616.

This is a very brief outline of the life of our greatest writer, for little more can be said of him with certainty, though the plays – and poems – are living witness to the wisdom, humanity and many-faceted nature of the man. He was both popular and successful as a dramatist, perhaps less so as an actor. He probably began work as a dramatist in the late 1580s, by collaborating with other playwrights and adapting old plays, and by 1598 Francis Meres was paying tribute to his excellence in both comedy and tragedy. His first original play was probably *Love's Labour's Lost* (1590) and while the theatres were closed during the plague he wrote his narrative poems *Venus and Adonis* (1593) and *The Rape of Lucrece* (1594). The sonnets were almost certainly written in the 1590s though not published until 1609; the first 126 are addressed to a young man who was his friend and patron, while the rest are concerned with the 'dark lady'.

The dating of Shakespeare's plays has exercised scholars ever since the publication of the First Folio (1623), which listed them as comedies, histories and tragedies. It seems more important to look at them chronologically as far as possible, in order to trace Shakespeare's considerable development as a dramatist. The first period, say to the middle of the 1590s, included such plays as *Love's Labour's Lost*, *The Comedy of Errors*, *Richard III*, *The Taming of the Shrew*, *Romeo and Juliet* and *Richard II*. These early plays embrace the categories listed in the First Folio, so that Shakespeare the craftsman is evident in his capacity for variety of subject and treatment. The next phase includes *A Midsummer's Night's Dream*, *The Merchant of Venice*, *Henry IV Parts 1 and 2*, *Henry V* and *Much Ado About Nothing*, as well as *Julius Caesar*, *As You Like It* and *Twelfth Night*. These are followed, in the early years of the century, by his great tragic period: *Hamlet*, *Othello*, *King Lear* and *Macbeth*, with *Antony and Cleopatra* and *Coriolanus* belonging to 1607–09. The final phase embraces the romances (1610–13), *Cymbeline*, *The Tempest* and *The Winter's Tale* and the historical play *Henry VIII*.

Each of these revision aids will place the individual text under examination in the chronology of the remarkable dramatic output that spanned twenty years from the early 1590s to about 1613. The practical theatre for which Shakespeare wrote and acted derived from the inn courtyards in which performances had taken place, the few playhouses in his day being modelled on their structure. They were circular or hexagonal in shape, allowing the balconies and boxes around the walls full view of the stage. This large stage, which had no scenery, jutted out into the pit, the most extensive part of the theatre, where the poorer people – the 'groundlings' – stood. There was no roof (though the Blackfriars, used from 1608 onwards, was an indoor theatre) and thus bad weather meant no performance. Certain plays were acted at court, and these private performances normally marked some special occasion. Costumes, often rich ones, were used, and music was a common feature, with musicians on or under the stage; this sometimes had additional features, for example a trapdoor to facilitate the entry of a ghost. Women were barred by law from appearing on stage, and all female parts were played by boy actors; this undoubtedly explains the many instances in Shakespeare where a woman has to conceal her identity by disguising

herself as a man, e.g. Rosalind in *As You Like It*, Viola in *Twelfth Night*.

Shakespeare and his contemporaries often adapted their plays from sources in history and literature, extending an incident or a myth or creating a dramatic narrative from known facts. They were always aware of their own audiences, and frequently included topical references, sometimes of a satirical flavour, which would appeal to – and be understood by – the groundlings as well as their wealthier patrons who occupied the boxes. Shakespeare obviously learned much from his fellow dramatists and actors, being on good terms with many of them. Ben Jonson paid generous tribute to him in the lines prefaced to the First Folio of Shakespeare's plays:

Thou art a monument without a tomb,
And art alive still, while thy book doth live
And we have wits to read, and praise to give.

Among his contemporaries were Thomas Kyd (1558–94) and Christopher Marlowe (1564–93). Kyd wrote *The Spanish Tragedy*, the revenge motif here foreshadowing the much more sophisticated treatment evident in *Hamlet*, while Marlowe evolved the 'mighty line' of blank verse, a combination of natural speech and elevated poetry. The quality and variety of Shakespeare's blank verse owes something to the innovatory brilliance of Marlowe but carries the stamp of individuality, richness of association, technical virtuosity and, above all, the genius of imaginative power.

The texts of Shakespeare's plays are still rich sources for scholars, and the editors of these revision aids have used the Arden editions of Shakespeare, which are regarded as pre-eminent for their scholarly approach. They are strongly recommended for advanced students, but other editions, like The New Penguin Shakespeare, The New Swan, The Signet are all good annotated editions currently available. A reading list of selected reliable works on the play being studied is provided at the end of each commentary and students are advised to turn to these as their interest in the play deepens.

Literary terms used in these notes

In the scene summaries, critical commentaries, textual notes and, particularly, in the sub-headings under *Style*, literary terms are used and defined (e.g. the section on *Dramatic Irony*). Consequently only a few are listed here.

Alliteration Words close together in a phrase or line which begin with the same letter: 'In *p*ractice let us *p*ut it *p*resently' (Act I, Scene 1); 'For a *h*awk, a *h*orse, or a *h*usband?' (Act III, Scene 4).

Antithesis Strictly, the opposite, the use of contrast or opposition, or the juxtaposition of contrasting ideas, words or phrases to produce an effect of balance: 'A bird of my tongue is better than a beast of yours' (Act I, Scene 1); 'She's too low for a high praise, too brown for a fair praise, and too little for a great praise' (Act I, Scene 1).

Metaphor A compressed comparison without the use of *like* or *as*: 'I had rather be a canker in a hedge than a rose in his grace' (Act I, Scene 3); 'Fetter strong madness in a silken thread' (Act V, Scene 1).

Simile A comparison using *like* or *as:* 'For look where Beatrice, like a lapwing, runs/Close by the ground to hear our conference.' (Act III, Scene 1); 'He is now as valiant as Hercules that only tells a lie and swears it.' (Act IV, Scene 1).

The play

Plot

Having suppressed a rebellion in his own principality organized by his illegitimate half-brother, Don John, Don Pedro, Prince of Aragon, arrives to stay in Messina with the Governor, Leonato. Two friends accompany him; Claudio, who has been distinguished by him because of his service in the war, and Benedick, a friend who soon resumes his 'merry war' of words with Leonato's niece, Beatrice. Claudio confesses that he has fallen in love with Hero, Leonato's daughter, and Don Pedro agrees to woo her on Claudio's behalf. Don John, meanwhile, and despite the fact that he has been reconciled to Don Pedro, tries to cause mischief by telling the masked Claudio that Don Pedro is courting Hero on his own account.

After Don Pedro has obtained Hero for Claudio, he, Leonato and Claudio devise a plot whereby Beatrice and Benedick overhear that each is in love with the other. Meanwhile Don John devises his own plot, or rather one of his followers, Borachio does, to discredit Hero by offering Claudio visual proof of her unfaithfulness. This is done off-stage but is effective, since Hero is denounced in church by an irate Claudio supported by Don Pedro. The Friar counsels that Hero be reported dead in order to bring Claudio to repentance. Meanwhile, the Watch overhear Borachio boasting to Conrade of what he has done and, despite the bungling of Dogberry, the two are arrested and Borachio confesses his crime.

Prior to this, Beatrice and Benedick had been drawn closer together by their common sympathy for Hero, and Benedick challenges Claudio to a duel. Leonato, angry on his daughter's account, also challenges Claudio, but when the Watch reveal the truth of the matter to Claudio, he repents the loss of Hero and agrees to marry Leonato's niece. Naturally she turns out to be Hero herself, and the play ends on a note of complete reconciliation with a double marriage, that of Claudio and Hero and of Beatrice and Benedick. Don John, who has fled, is caught and the play ends in a light-hearted manner.

Sources

There is no single source for *Much Ado About Nothing*, and it seems likely that Shakespeare drew on a number of literary sources – as well as his own imagination – for the plot and plots of the play. The deceived lover is a commonplace of literary history, and two marked instances of which Shakespeare may have known occur in the epics of Ariosto and Spenser. Ariosto's *Orlando Furioso* (1516) was translated into English verse by Sir John Harington (1591), the lovers in the fifth canto being Ariodante and Genevra. In Edmund Spenser's *The Faerie Queene* (1590) (Book II Canto 4) the lovers are Phedon and Claribell. Phedon is betrayed by his close friend Philemon, the latter persuading Claribell's maid to disguise herself as Claribell and receive him, Philemon, as her lover. Phedon sees this and afterwards kills Claribell and poisons Philemon, who (like Don John) acts from evil motives.

A primary source appears to be the twenty-second story of *La Prima Parte de la Novelle* (1554) of the Italian writer Matteo Bandello, which was translated into French and English. Here Timbreo falls in love with Fenicia, daughter of Lionato (note Timbreo is from Aragon, Lionato resides in Messina). But Girondo, Timbreo's friend, also falls in love with Fenicia, and says that he will show Timbreo that Fenicia is unfaithful to him. Girondo's servant disguised as a gentleman enters Fenicia's bedroom observed by Timbreo, who breaks off the engagement. Fenicia is near death but revives and is secreted away to the country. Reports of her death are put out and a poem is inscribed on her tomb. Girondo repents his evil and confesses all to Timbreo. Timbreo forgives him, they vindicate Fenicia's reputation, and the latter – who has been renamed Lucilla – grows in beauty as time passes. Lionato tells Timbreo that he has found a bride for him. Timbreo marries Lucilla – really Fenicia – and Girondo marries her younger sister. All is forgiven, reconciliation is effected, and King Piero of Aragon receives the couples on their return to Messina with lavish entertainment. Shakespeare's adaptions and derivations, as well as alterations, are given below (see *Treatment of sources*).

Thus far sources, or at least the main ones, for the main plot. The sub-plot involving Beatrice and Benedick is part of a general tradition in the Renaissance which has rejection of love by courtiers and witty characters as one of its main themes. Shakespeare adapts and uses this tradition in his own plays, *The Two Gentlemen of Verona* and, more particularly, in *The Taming of the Shrew*. Beatrice herself is recognizably of the same quality – but of course with differences – as Rosalind, in *As You Like It* (who satirizes affected love) and Portia, in *The Merchant of Venice*, who itemizes and derides her suitors as they arrive to take the casket test. Benedick derives from Berowne in *Love's Labour's Lost*, for Berowne turns everything to wit and in turn is changed into a lover to his own self-confusion. Dogberry also seems to have his source in his own creator's plays, with Dull *(Love's Labour's Lost)*, Bottom *(A Midsummer Night's Dream)* and Lancelot Gobbo *(The Merchant of Venice)* being his most obvious antecedents.

Treatment of sources

It will be seen from the previous section that the plot of Shakespeare's *Much Ado About Nothing* employs many of the settings and situations of Bandello's story. Messina is the location in both, with slight changes the names of Don Pedro and Leonato are derived from it, while Claudio's service in war is the equivalent of Timbreo's. The latter employed a friend to get Lionato's consent to the marriage, which again is an approximation to Don Pedro's 'courtship' of Hero. Girondo gets someone in disguise to demonstrate Fenicia's disloyalty (cf Margaret in *Much Ado About Nothing*). Timbreo denounces Fenicia just as Claudio denounces Hero, Fenicia is presumed dead while Hero's death is proclaimed, and in both story and play there is ritual mourning with verses. Timbreo agrees, like Claudio, to accept the bride nominated for him and, as with Hero, she turns out to be the bride he was originally to marry. Story and play end with celebrations.

Thus far we are close to Bandello, though in the actual story there are many differences which it would be pedantic to refer to here. Shakespeare, however, made a number of alterations which were chiefly in the interests of unity of action, or parallelism, or contrast. Thus Bandello's story occupies a period of about a year or so, whereas Shakespeare condenses the action of his play into a few days. This enhances the dramatic immediacy of the play, ensures swiftness of movement and unity of action. The time sequence is as follows. On the first day Don Pedro and his friends arrive, the supper in their honour being held the same night. The masked dance after the supper allows Don Pedro to undertake the courtship of Hero on behalf of Claudio. Don John proposes to 'cross it', and Don Pedro initiates the plot to ultimately get Beatrice and Benedick together in marriage – there is of course no equivalent to this in Bandello. This takes us up to Act II Scene 2. The next day the plan to gull Benedick is carried out and this is followed – perhaps paralleled – by the duping of Beatrice. At night, off-stage, there is another deception, initiated by Borachio, with Margaret as Hero, Don John having already advertised Hero's disloyalty to Claudio and Don Pedro. After this the Watch are given their instructions – such as they are – by Dogberry, and subsequently arrest Borachio and Conrade. This takes us to the end of Act III Scene 3.

There follows the intended wedding day, with Leonato instructing the Watch to examine their prisoners, Claudio's public condemnation of Hero, Benedick's challenge to Claudio. Conrade and Borachio are brought before Leonato, Don John's plot is revealed – we also learn that he has fled – and Beatrice and Benedick confess their love. At night on this third day Claudio sings his epitaph to Hero, who was supposed to have been buried on the same day that she died, and agrees to marry Antonio's daughter. This takes up to Act V Scene 3. On the fourth day the play ends with the weddings and celebrations. These days of action are not necessarily successive days, since we remember that Leonato had said (Act II, Scene 1) that the wedding of Claudio and Hero could not take place for a week. Act II Scene 3 cannot therefore be given a certain time, since it could have taken place on any day in the week before the wedding. This is balanced by Act III Scene 2, in which Don John accuses Hero, which surely closely follows Act II Scene 2, when the plan to discredit her was devised. Of course, this may be a slip on Shakespeare's part, or it could even be that Leonato changed his mind about the date of the wedding.

Some of Shakespeare's characters, as we have seen, either do not feature in Bandello or have a somewhat different function. Don Pedro has a major role in *Much Ado* from his first entrance to the rounding-off festivities, but Don Piero in Bandello's story has no plot functions to perform. Other differences are that Fenicia has a mother, Hero does not; Claudio is more gullible than Timbreo, the latter being largely jealous whereas Claudio believes, twice, that Don Pedro is courting Hero for himself. Given that she is of lower birth, Timbreo is happy to seduce Fenicia before deciding to marry her whereas Claudio is diffident and honourable (at least in the sexual sense) towards Hero, as these two are of equal status. There is no rival for Hero's love as there is in Bandello and the jealousy motif is found in the person of Don John for Don Pedro and Claudio but not apparently because he covets Hero himself. Don Pedro *and* Claudio witness the Borachio-Margaret exchange and not just the lover alone as in Bandello. Timbreo employs a friend to break off the engagement to Fenicia, while Claudio's accusations in church are much more tellingly dramatic. Whereas Timbreo doubts his judgement of Fenicia, Claudio never doubts his of Hero. Perhaps the most brilliant departure is that whereas in Bandello the emphasis is on God, who will ultimately clear Fenicia, in *Much Ado* there is the superb bungling comedy of the Watch discovering the truth. Timbreo has redeeming even sympathetic qualities, but Claudio has few if any, and this heightens the potentially tragic effect. Shakespeare restricts the scenes of his play just as he restricts the time, and obviously this leads to a much greater unity. Bandello takes his action from Messina to a country house, but *Much Ado About Nothing* has its whole action in the Messina of Leonato's palace, the street outside, the church and gaol.

The additional characters who do not derive from Bandello tend to dominate *Much Ado About Nothing*. I am referring to Benedick and Beatrice and of course Dogberry. The solution of the plot through the bumbling intervention of Dogberry and his associates is Shakespeare's invention, though it may have derived in part from a letter written by Lord Burleigh to Walsingham when a plot was feared against the queen. This gives some account of a Watch at Enfield which, like Dogberry's, did not seem likely at sight to 'reprehend' any miscreants. As for Beatrice and Benedick, these are elevated by Shakespeare to the centre of our interest. Strangely, two characters in Bandello's story are married at the same time as the two leading characters. This scene may have given Shakespeare the idea which he so richly expanded. The idea of the low comedy of the Watch and the high sophisticated comedy of Beatrice and Benedick forms an admirable contrast – see the section on *Structure and style* later in this commentary – and shows Shakespeare's awareness of the aesthetic structure of his play. In a sense the plot is the least important part of *Much Ado About Nothing*. Shakespeare's triumph is manifold; it is in characterization, dramatic (and comic) immediacy, language (and particularly poetry) and a number of other areas which underline his genius. He has the capacity to transform outlines of improbability into what is real and lifelike. His insight conveys the conception of life which the artist has as a whole. A story with a realistic plot can be lifeless if its characters are not fully realized; a poor or improbable plot comes to life when it is invested with real characters. Shakespeare is often somewhat casual in his plots; it is in his *use* of plot that he shows his imagination.

The plot of *Much Ado About Nothing* sometimes creaks. Consider how it is dependent upon what is overheard, and in one instance on what is supposedly seen; but such is the pace of the action that we accept it all. There is little time for thought as we watch. Improbability and deception are followed by wit, knockabout humour, or the serious effects of a plot against virtue. Shakespeare's sources, whether major ones like Bandello, whether a tradition of anti-love, whether knowledge of a Watch being formed to deal with a given contingency, all become transformed under the hands of imaginative genius.

Date and title

Meres's entry in the *Stationer's Register* in 1598, which contains a list of important works, does not give *Much Ado About Nothing*. It seems likely that a date after that, probably late in the same year, is possible, since the famous actor Will Kemp played Dogberry according to the *Quarto* of 1600, but left the theatre company which produced the play early in 1599.

Richard White observed that the Elizabethan pronunciation of 'noting' and 'nothing' was much the same, and that the play is about 'noting' – listening, observing, eavesdropping. Benedick, Beatrice and Claudio note what they hear and see, but it rests upon nothing though, certainly, there is 'Much Ado' in terms of gulling and much more serious ado in the church scene. *As You Like It* and the subtitle of *Twelfth Night; or, what you will* are throw-away titles in the same tradition, and represent a witty and perhaps slightly satirical glance by Shakespeare at his own craft.

Scene summaries, critical comment, textual notes and revision questions

Act I Scene 1

Leonato, governor of Messina, receives a letter telling him that Don Pedro, Prince of Aragon and his followers are returning that night, after military engagement, to stay with him. In this party are Claudio, a count from Florence who, though young, has distinguished himself on the battlefield, and Benedick, a nobleman from Padua. Beatrice, the governor's niece, is most disparaging about Benedick, and when he arrives they resume what is evidently a long-standing battle of words. Don Pedro announces his intention of staying for at 'least a month' and this news is welcomed by Leonato. Indeed he extends an invitation to the whole party, including Don John, the Prince's brother, the pair having become reconciled after the recent 'action'. Claudio reveals his romantic interest in Hero, Leonato's daughter, firstly to Benedick, and then to Don Pedro. Benedick ridicules the whole idea of love and marriage while Don Pedro offers to disguise himself as Claudio and to woo Hero for him.

Commentary

All the principal characters are introduced and the first strand in the deception plot is proposed when Don Pedro affects to assume Claudio's identity. Leonato appears kind and hospitable, Don Pedro courteous and decisive; notice the wit and sharpness of Beatrice (but note that her first question is about Benedick), while Benedick plays the 'obstinate heretic' wittily (and note that he has observed that Beatrice exceeds Hero in beauty). So far Don John is not a man of many words, and Hero is of fewer still. The 'merry war' between Beatrice and Benedick – concealing perhaps a need for each other – is here resumed and is an important part of the play. Note the word-play, the wit, the punning, the incidence of sexual innuendo. The background is sketched in and there is an easy atmosphere between the families. There is a careful structuring of blank verse and prose: the latter occupying the scene to take in the early reportage and the needling exchanges between Beatrice and Benedick, the blank verse fittingly used to convey the elevated feelings of early love experienced by Claudio (though he has already confided these feelings in prose to the sceptical Benedict). Further critical points are noted below.

by this i.e. by this time.
achiever . . . full numbers Winner . . . few casualties.
remembered Recognized, deserving of praise.
figure Appearance.
better bettered Exceeded to a greater extent.
modest . . . badge of bitterness This is a mark. Servants often wore an emblem indicating the house they served and their own modest status.
kind Natural.
joy at weeping i.e. indulge being miserable.
Mountanto A name derived from the fencing term *montanto*, meaning an upward thrust or blow.
sort Rank.
pleasant Entertaining.
bills Posters.
flight Light arrow.
subscribed i.e. signed his name in acceptance of the challenge.
bird-bolt Blunt headed arrow used by bird-catchers.
killed and eaten i.e. boasted about his feats in battle.
eat all of his killing Beatrice is implying that he hasn't killed anybody.
tax Criticize severely.
meet with Equal to (with a pun on 'meat' associated with 'eating').
musty victual Stale food.
holp Helped.
trencher-man i.e. having a huge appetite.
stomach Digestion.
to a lady This is typical Beatrice wit. She plays on 'too' implying that Benedict 'serves' the opposite sex, i.e. makes love.
lord i.e. can he serve his superiors?
A lord . . . a lord i.e. Benedick treats his superiors as equals.
stuffed (a) filled (b) dummy-like.
stuffing Beatrice is using sexual innuendo, implying (a) that what Benedick is filled with is useless and (b) that his sexual performance is inadequate.
gets . . . that i.e. wins nothing in the skirmish.
five wits These reflect the five senses of hearing, sight, smell, taste and touch.
halting off i.e. limped away.
bear i.e. carry heraldic arms.
a difference i.e. an alteration or addition to a coat of arms to distinguish a junior branch from the main line of the family.
all the wealth The only possession.
be . . . creature Show that he is capable of reason.
sworn brother Companions in arms were bound by oath to support each other.

faith Oath, obligation.
block Mould (for shaping a hat).
books List of approved people.
and If.
study Beatrice is continuing the 'books' analogy.
squarer Swaggerer.
pestilence Plague.
taker Victim.
presently Immediately.
hold friends i.e. shake hands (and still be friends).
run mad i.e. catch the disease (ironic in view of the ultimate coming
  together of Beatrice and Benedick).
is approached Has arrived.
meet your trouble? i.e. the cost of entertaining us?
encounter Welcome.
charge Responsibility of entertaining.
Were you in doubt . . . her? Notice the witty (and somewhat impertinent)
  emphasis of Benedick's first words.
full Straight.
fathers herself Shows her parentage in her looks.
have . . . shoulders i.e. wish to have his white hair or bald head.
marks Pays attention to.
Lady Disdain Her contemptuous air is referred to on a number of
  occasions; judging from her reply, she rather enjoys being thought of in
  this way.
meet Fitting.
dear happiness Stroke of luck.
pernicious Wicked.
cold blood Calm, unmoved nature.
humour Disposition.
still Always.
scape Escape.
predestinate Fated to happen.
rare Superb.
parrot-teacher i.e. she repeats herself, just like a parrot repeats words it
  hears.
A bird of my tongue . . . yours i.e. speaking as I do is better than being
  dumb (like a horse and you).
continuer i.e. had your stamina.
keep your way Carry on as you wish.
jade's i.e. belonging to a worthless horse (which is up to 'tricks' and
  difficult to control).
occasion Reason.
forsworn Guilty of breaking an oath.
noted . . . not Did not find her particularly worthy of notice.
modest Decorous, well-conducted.
a professed tyrant i.e. someone who is known for his sexual conquests.

low Short (note the witty quibble on 'high').

brown Dark-haired (and note the quibble on 'fair').

commendation Praise.

in sport i.e. joking.

sad Serious.

flouting Jack Mocking fellow.

hare-finder Finding a hare in grass or undergrowth needs good eye-sight: Cupid was blind.

Vulcan Roman god of metal-working.

go in the song i.e. be in harmony with your mood.

matter Thing.

fury Temper.

wear his cap with suspicion i.e. to wear a cap to cover the horns attributed to husbands whose wives have been unfaithful.

threescore i.e. sixty (will no one survive to be a bachelor at that age?).

Go to Carry on then.

print Imprint, mark.

sign away Sundays Be miserable at home on Sundays.

constrain Force.

charge . . . allegiance Command you because of the duty you owe me as your lord.

secret i.e. silent (about what has passed between us).

the old tale i.e. however strongly Claudio denies the truth of this, there is no doubting the proof.

fetch me in Draw me out.

By my troth Upon my word.

my two . . . troths A reference to his loyalty to Don Pedro and Claudio.

fire . . . stake A contemporary reference to the fact that heretics were burnt at the stake.

in the despite of Contemptuously disregarding.

in the force of his will Wilfully.

recheat This is a call on the hunting horn to rally the hounds.

winded Blown.

baldrick A belt worn from one shoulder across the chest to support the other. The sense of the passage seems to be that he will not risk cuckoldry, either publicly known or secretly suspected.

the fine The conclusion.

the finer i.e. the better dressed.

look pale with love This is a fine anticipation of what ultimately happens to Benedick.

with drinking i.e. a flush from drinking too much alcohol.

a ballad-maker's pen A scornful allusion to sentimental ballads of love and the loved one.

sign of a blind Cupid The various trades and professions had signs hung up to advertise their wares – hence Cupid as god of love would signal a brothel.

notable argument Standing example for discussion.

hang . . . cat These are references to cats in baskets being used as archery targets.

Adam Adam Bell was an outlaw in a ballad. He was famous as an archer.

as time shall try Proverbial 'As time will tell'.

bear the yoke Submit to domestication.

vilely Crudely.

signify Indicate, advertise.

horn-mad Enraged.

spent . . . quiver Used up all his arrows.

Venice Notorious for its fashionable prostitutes.

quake Shiver: with a pun on 'quiver'.

earthquake i.e. that is what it will take to make me quake.

temporize . . . hours Negotiate to gain time.

repair Go.

fail him Let him down (by not going).

matter Ability (Benedick is being sarcastic).

embassage Mission.

commit . . . Benedick This is a run of the conventional phrases used in letter writing.

sometime guarded (a) accompanied protectively (b) embroidered.

guards Trimmings.

basted Sewn lightly.

old ends (a) traditional endings to lettters (see above) (b) remnants of material (c) conventional values.

may do me good i.e. help me.

apt Ready.

affect Love.

rougher task i.e. the business of fighting.

liking . . . love i.e. inklings of the way I felt.

prompting Indicating.

presently Soon.

book of words Too much talk.

break with Break the news to.

twist Spin.

minister i.e. treat by healing.

complexion Appearance.

salv'd Remedied.

treatise Narrative.

What . . . flood? Why do more than is necessary?

The fairest . . . necessity The most suitable gift is the one that is needed.

Look . . . fit If it serves the purpose it's the right thing.

'tis once Briefly.

fit Supply.

encounter Style of telling, a metaphor from the fighting that has just ended.

Act I Scene 2

Leonato meets Antonio, his brother. The latter reveals that a servant has overheard Don Pedro speak of his love for Hero to Claudio. According to the servant he intends to tell Hero of his love that night, and if he finds her responsive to it, to approach her father immediately. Leonato is not wholly convinced but decides that Hero should be warned in case the rumour is true.

Commentary

This brief scene provides the first piece of unintentional misinformation arising from overheard conversation; it contrasts effectively with the deliberate misinformation, as a result of plotting, which is going to cause the 'much ado' of the play's title. Ironically it places Hero in the role of potential victim, whereas later, as the result of deception, she will be the victim.

Are they good? Is it good? – news was a plural.
event Occasion.
stamps Imprints itself on.
cover i.e. as of a book.
thick-pleached With densely-interwoven branches.
alley Avenue.
orchard Garden.
discovered Revealed.
accordant In agreement, receptive.
take ... the top Seize the opportunity.
wit Sense.
appear itself Becomes apparent, materializes.
withal Nevertheless.
peradventure By any chance.
cry you mercy Beg your pardon.

Act I Scene 3

Don John rejects the advice of his companion Conrade, who advocates common sense. Don John has recently rebelled, been defeated and then conditionally pardoned by his brother. He does not hide his intention to continue vengeful and unco-operative. Borachio, another of his followers, arrives to report that he has overheard Don Pedro agreeing to woo Hero on his own account and then give her to Claudio. Don John feels that this may provide the opportunity for him to undertake some mischief with the help of the other two, and they leave belatedly to join in the festivities.

Commentary

Don John reveals that there is malice in his nature, hence his depression at not being in the forefront of things and dependent on his brother, while Conrade reveals his cunning in suggesting that Don John adapts himself to circumstances. Don John's obsessive bitterness is disconcerting, and both he and Conrade draw on nature: Don John to show how twisted his own is 'a canker in a hedge', Conrade to advise cunning and deception 'it is needful that you frame the season for your own harvest'. With Borachio's news of the 'intended marriage' Don John finds a focus for his malice, since he is jealous of Claudio and sees an opportunity to undermine the man who has displaced him in his brother's favour. Borachio appears as a born rogue and opportunist and this, the second report of the conversation between Don Pedro and Claudio, makes for suspense as we wait to see what Don John will do.

What the good-year An exclamation similar to 'What on earth!'
out of measure Beyond limit.
the occasion that breeds The situation that is developing.
present Immediate.
sufferance Endurance.
born under Saturn Astrologically, people born under this sign would incline to the gloomy and morose outlook.
goest about Tries hard.
moral medicine . . . mortifying mischief Philosophical cure to a fatal disease.
stomach Appetite.
tend on Attend to.
claw Flatter.
full show Display.
controlment Restriction.
newly Once more.
take true root A gardening metaphor meaning 'become established'.
fair weather i.e. good conditions for developing.
frame the season i.e. do what is necessary at the time.
harvest Result of your actions (note the sequence of imagery from nature).
canker (a) dog rose (b) plant disease.
blood (a) disposition (b) illegitimacy.
fashion a carriage Alter, transform my customary conduct.
trusted . . . muzzle i.e. allowed my head yet restrained from biting.
enfranchised with a clog Freed from slavery but still shackled to a block.
decreed Decided.

intelligence News.
model Plan.
What . . . unquietness? What kind of a fool is he who courts disturbance?
Marry An oath meaning 'By the Virgin Mary'.
most exquisite Note the contempt and envy in the tone.
proper squire Worthy young gallant (again the tone is sarcastic).
Which way looks he? Whom has he chosen?
forward March-chick! The reference is to a young bird which has been hatched early, and alludes to Claudio, whom Don John regards as precocious and impertinent.
to this i.e. to learn this.
entertained for Employed as.
perfumer One who uses fumes or incense.
smoking Fumigating, as a way of disinfecting.
sad Serious.
whipped me Moved myself quickly.
arras Hanging tapestry screen.
start-up Upstart.
my overthrow Perhaps this is an indication of the fact that the rebellion had been led by Don John.
cross Thwart, frustrate, with a quibble on 'make the sign of the cross'.
bless myself Call myself happy, with a quibble which balances the previous reference.
sure Trustworthy.
their cheer . . . I am subdued i.e. my defeat gives them added reason to celebrate.
Would the cook . . . The general meaning is that if the cook felt like him – Don John – he would poison all of them.
prove Find out.

Revision questions on Act I

1 Write an account of the 'merry war' between Beatrice and Benedick in this Act.
2 Write brief character sketches of (a) Don Pedro (b) Claudio (c) Leonato (d) Don John.
3 Write an essay on appearance and reality in this Act.
4 Show how dramatic expectation is aroused in this Act.
5 Examine any sequences of images which you find important in Act I.

Act II Scene 1

At Leonato's house, after the meal, Beatrice is wittily defending her views on men and marriage. The dancers enter, the first couple being Hero and the masked Don Pedro, who are conversing charmingly and wittily. Next come Balthazar, Don Pedro's attendant, and Margaret, one of Hero's gentlewomen, who is more than a match for him. Ursula, another of Hero's gentlewomen, and the elderly Antonio make up the third couple, with Antonio failing to conceal his true identity although he is masked. Lastly come Beatrice and Benedick. He claims that he is only repeating insulting remarks which he has heard about her while she, affecting not to know with whom she is dancing, mocks Benedick's wit. Don John and Borachio sow the seeds of doubt in Claudio's mind concerning Don Pedro's real intentions, saying that he (Don Pedro) is to marry Hero that very night. Benedick believes that Don Pedro has indeed 'stolen' Hero, and taunts Claudio before reproaching the Prince. Don Pedro explains to Benedick what he has really done but then goads him to an outburst vilifying Beatrice, whose entrance causes Benedick to leave. The Prince reassures Claudio that 'I have wooed in thy name' and that Hero and her father are agreeable. Arrangements for the marriage are discussed and, at Don Pedro's instigation, plans are laid to bring about a match between Beatrice and Benedick.

Commentary

Beatrice's discussion of Don John enables her to exercise her verbal wit at the expense of him and of Benedick, but she also reveals a superb addiction to sexual word-play. She dominates the early exchanges of this scene by sheer force of ingenuity and imaginative repartee, even anticipating the coming dance with her witty suggestions to Hero about the latter's imminent courtship. The assumption of the masks is a deliberate underlining of the appearance and reality theme which characterizes the play. There is a careful structural pairing, first of Balthazar and Margaret (brief witty exchanges), Ursula and Antonio (the latter pathetic in denying his identity) and Beatrice and Benedick, each intent on baiting the other, the dance and masking enabling them to pretend they do not recognize each other. Of course they do, and this sharpens their wit and makes the inflicted injuries the more hurtful, though it is part of the 'merry war'.

Dramatically the scene is effective because the watchers contribute to the plot, Don John cunningly accosting Claudio by the name of Benedick in order to undermine his faith in Don

Pedro's integrity. Claudio's impressionable nature is shown by his reaction (in romantic and self-indulgent verse), and his lack of trust is anticipated here. His later response to Hero's 'infidelity' casts him, as here, in an unsympathetic light. There is a certain cruelty in Benedick's extension of Claudio's torment, and he himself underlines the revenge motif of Don John by swearing to be revenged on Beatrice for what she has said. Don Pedro's honesty is soon revealed, but Benedick's rhetoric in condemnation of Beatrice covers a wide range of imagery, though even this is extended when he makes an elaborate and wordy exit on Beatrice's approach (obviously he is still very offended with her). Beatrice's witty innuendo gives way to genuine joy at the love of Claudio and Hero; it is an anticipation of her own later genuine joy in her love for Benedick. She affects to feel out of things by not having a husband herself, and flirts with Don Pedro, at least verbally. Her deprivation motivates Don Pedro to think of bringing her together with Benedick, an important decision for the plot. Even Hero is involved, and it is a measure of her affection for Beatrice that she wishes to see her happily married. Note the parallelism, which has the overt marriage plan for Claudio and Hero (though achieved by the subterfuge of Don Pedro's courtship) and the covert plan of marriage for Beatrice and Benedict which is going to play such a major part in the deception/reality issues on which the play turns.

tartly Sharply, sourly.
heart-burned Suffering from indigestion.
if a If he.
By my troth See note p.21.
shrewd Sharp (but note the pun on 'shrew' – a woman who never stops nagging and berating her husband).
curst (a) awkward (b) cursed, with perhaps a play on 'curt', meaning 'shortened' – here short-tempered.
sending Gift.
Just Correctly, exactly.
husband i.e. to whom she can give 'horns' by being unfaithful.
at him Persistently asking him.
in the woollen Between rough blankets.
light on Find.
in earnest As part payment.
bearward i.e. the bear or animal-keeper.
lead his apes into hell This follows on from the previous image. It is supposed to be the proverbial fate of old maids.
for the heavens i.e. to be admitted into Heaven.
ruled Governed.

make curtsy Show respect.
fitted Supplied.
metal Material.
overmastered Dominated by.
dust According to Genesis, 2,7, man was 'formed of the dust of the ground'.
clod of wayward marl Lump of clay.
match in my kindred Marry within the family.
in that kind As a suitor.
in good time (a) without unseemly haste (b) to the accompaniment of the correct rhythm (an anticipation of the dance to come).
important Importunate, pressing.
measure (a) moderation (b) rhythm.
measure Slow, grave dance.
cinque-pace Lively dance, from the French 'five steps'.
first suit i.e. the wooing.
full as fantastical Just as energetic in movement.
mannerly-modest Well-conducted and respectable.
ancientry Tradition.
bad legs i.e. ageing and tiring.
sink Note the pun with 'cinque'.
apprehend . . . shrewdly Grasp the matter with true insight.
can . . . daylight Beatrice is saying that she knows a church means marriage.
good Plenty of.
bout Turn, circuit.
so Provided that.
favour Appearance.
defend Forbid.
lute . . . case Presumably Don Pedro is wearing a grotesque mask, compared here to the case which would hold the lute.
visor Face-mask.
Philemon's . . . Jove The latter, the chief of the Roman gods, came down to earth disguised as a poor traveller. He was given shelter by a peasant, Philemon, and his wife, after he had been refused shelter elsewhere.
thatch'd i.e. like Philemon's hut.
clerk The priest's clerk led the responses in church services.
counterfeit Imitate.
ill-well i.e. look so bad yet do such a good imitation.
dry hand i.e. too old for love.
up and down All over, in every detail.
excellent wit This is heavy sarcasm at the old man's expense.
mum Be quiet.
good wit The pick of my humorous remarks.
'Hundred Merry Tales' Well-known book of simple funny stories.
the Prince's jester Note that this would diminish Benedick's position.

dull Slow-witted.

only his gift . . . slanders His only talent is in making up unbelievable, maliciously false reports.

libertines Dissolute characters, originally freed slaves.

commendation Praise.

villainy Rudeness, punning perhaps on the other meaning of slavery and bondage.

fleet Company.

boarded Came alongside and engaged in hostilities (with a strong sexual implication).

break a comparison Waste an unflattering simile, as jousters break lances when they don't hit the mark squarely.

peradventure See note p23.

marked See note p20.

withdrawn Taken aside.

visor i.e. masked man.

Are . . . Benedick? An index to Don John's cunning – he knows quite well that he is addressing Claudio.

You may do the part i.e. act honourably.

banquet Dessert, usually of fruit, sweetmeats and wine.

office Undertaking.

faith . . . blood Reliability is overpowerd by emotion, continuing the 'bewitching' metaphor.

accident Event.

hourly proof Demonstrated every hour.

mistrusted Suspected.

willow The symbol of grief in love.

County Count.

usurer's chain Money-lenders, in common with other successful merchants, often wore elaborate chains as evidence of their wealth.

lieutenant's scarf A sash worn by the representative of the civil governor of a county.

honest drover Blunt and surly like a cattle-dealer.

so In that way.

sedges Rushes.

apt Likely.

that puts the world into her person i.e. attributes her own opinions to people in general.

gives me out Presents me publicly.

as I may When I can.

Lady Fame Something like 'Dame Rumour'.

a lodge in a warren A simple hut for use during the hunting season, probably located in an area set aside for breeding game.

flat transgression Downright sin.

a trust i.e. trusting.

had . . . amiss Would not have been out of order if.

their . . . saying i.e. they do as you say.

misused Abused.

past the endurance of a block! i.e. even a piece of wood would have reacted!

assume life i.e. shake, as if alive.

scold Quarrel.

not . . . myself Not knowing who I was.

duller . . . thaw i.e. drab and uninteresting, with nowhere to go because of the impassable roads.

huddling Heaping.

conveyance The action of transferring.

mark Target.

poniards Daggers.

terminations Terms.

she were endowed with i.e. her dowry was.

all . . . transgressed i.e. the whole of Creation.

Hercules As a punishment, he was condemned by the Oracle to serve one year as a slave.

turned spit i.e. undertake the most menial task in the kitchen.

cleft Split.

Ate The daughter of Zeus, who treacherously led men and gods into error and wrong-doing.

scholar One who had studied the classical languages. Latin was the language of exorcism.

conjure Convey away by magic.

perturbation Disorder.

Antipodes The other side of the world.

toothpicker i.e. the most insignificant thing.

Prester John A legendary Christian priest and Eastern ruler of the Middle Ages.

Cham's The khan's or emperor's. Kubla Khan is usually thought of as the Great Cham.

harpy A destructive mythological creature with a woman's face and body and a bird's wings and claws.

dish . . . Lady Tongue Food – with a pun on 'tongue' – meat as well as talk.

use Interest (Beatrice seems to be saying that Benedick gave her his heart once, and although she returned his affection in double measure, he proved untrue).

false dice i.e. trickery, deception.

put him down Degraded, upset him.

So I would not he should do me Because I do not wish him to do that to me – put me down (both degrade me and sleep with me).

civil Polite. This was also the Elizabethan spelling of 'Seville', a bitter orange, hence the pun.

jealous complexion i.e. yellow.

blazon Description.

conceit Understanding.

all grace i.e. God.

cue Note Beatrice's sarcasm as she uses this metaphor from the theatre.

dote Become foolish through love.

fool Innocent thing.

the windy side of care i.e. to windward, the right side to drive care away.

ear . . . heart Note Beatrice's improvised word-play.

alliance i.e. of families in marriage.

sunburnt Not fair-skinned, and therefore less marriageable.

'Heigh-ho' An expression of disappointment, and here one of self-pity.

getting Begetting, punning on 'get'.

got Begot (as above).

out o' question Without doubt.

a star danced i.e. astrologically influenced her personality.

out of suit i.e. puts off those who are courting her (by her mockery).

were Would be.

time goes on crutches i.e. time passes slowly.

rites Rituals (but with a pun on conjugal 'right').

just seven-night Only a week.

answer my mind Done what I have in mind.

breathing Breathing space.

one of Hercules' labours The classical hero noted for his immense strength and courage. He had to perform twelve labours.

fain Gladly.

fashion it Bring it about.

watchings Staying awake.

unhopefullest i.e. not the most hopeless.

strain Descent.

approved Proven.

confirmed honesty Unquestionable honour.

practise on Plot against.

in despite of Notwithstanding.

queasy stomach i.e. easily upset temperamentally.

Cupid Cupid's golden arrows caused love, his leaden ones, hate.

my drift The direction of my thoughts in this matter.

Act II Scene 2

Borachio reveals to Don John his plot to make Hero appear unfaithful and thereby trick Claudio into cancelling the wedding. The plot involves passing off Margaret as Hero, with the deception that 'Hero' is in love with him, Borachio.

Commentary

Notice the parallelism in the scenes: in the previous one we have seen a plot to make a marriage, whereas here is one to mar a projected marriage. Note the villainy of Don John and the cunning of Borachio, but also the sick or black comedy element which has now entered the plot. Note also a strand of improbability, since the deception would involve the disloyalty of Margaret to Hero, or the deceiving of Margaret herself.

cross Oppose, thwart.
bar Obstruction.
medicinable Medicinal, able to cure.
athwart Across the course of.
ranges evenly with Runs in the same direction as.
covertly Secretly.
unseasonable instant i.e. at any time however inconvenient.
appoint Arrange for.
What life . . . death What is the essential value of that (in helping to bring about the 'death' of a marriage).
temper Deal with, bring about.
mightily hold up i.e. stress in praising.
contaminated stale Corrupt (even diseased) prostitute.
undo Put an end to.
despite Spite.
meet hour Appropriate time.
intend Pretend.
zeal Ardent feeling of indignation.
cozened with Cheated by.
semblance of a maid i.e. the appearance of an innocent girl.
trial Proof.
instances Examples.
bear . . . than Carry no less promise of success than.
jealousy Suspicion.
the preparation overthrown i.e. the arrangements for the wedding.
Grow this However this may turn out.
ducats Gold or silver coins.
Be you constant . . . me Provided that you maintain the allegation, my cunning will bring about success.

Act II Scene 3

The scene opens with Benedick's private contemplation of Claudio's new found love. He considers the possibility of himself succumbing to love, but is interrrupted by the advent of

Claudio, Don Pedro and Leonato. They affect not to notice Benedick, but in reality are making sure that he overhears their report that Beatrice harbours a secret passion for him, Benedick. They subsequently discuss his faults and his virtues convincingly, aided and abetted by Hero and Leonato. When Beatrice is sent for to fetch him in to dinner, Benedick has already reassessed his position. Although Beatrice's responses are negative, Benedick convinces himself that these could be interpreted favourably, and decides to woo her.

Commentary

Benedick's contemplation is the first soliloquy of the play. His own wit is employed at the expense of Claudio, but there is more than a hint that he himself fears involvement. His definition of the ideal woman who is fair, wise, virtuous, and has all the graces ironically fits Beatrice. There is a fine dramatic stroke when Don Pedro and Claudio begin the duping of Benedick with Balthazar setting up the situation through a romantic song. This song is also ironic, with its implication that men are deceivers – in this play Hero will appear to be the deceiver.

The comedy of dual interaction is soon established, with Benedick's responses to what he overhears delivered to the audience while Don Pedro, Leonato and Claudio verbalize their plan. Perhaps the finest touch in this scene comes when Benedick suspects that this is a 'gull'. However, he dismisses the idea (as his vanity wishes him to) on the grounds that Leonato is old and respectable – and respected – and would not indulge in such duplicity. The account of Beatrice's supposed infatuation is graphic, witty, voluble in its exaggeration, to the point that Hero believes her to be so far gone as to die of it! Imagery of 'this fish will bite', of infection, of spreading 'the same net' for Beatrice all reinforce the 'sport'.

Benedick's second soliloquy shows just how he has been caught. We note him repeating 'fair, wise, virtuous' and this time applying them directly to Beatrice. Her entrance sparks off a brief exchange redolent of dramatic irony, Benedick looking for the 'double meaning' in what she says, unaware of the 'double' way in which his friends have used him. Yet there is a certain poignancy here. We suspect that both Benedick and Beatrice, skilful in verbal duels, are vulnerable to real emotional experience.

behaviours i.e. all his actions.

argument Subject.

the drum and the fife i.e. martial music.

the tabor and the pipe i.e. dancing music.

carving the fashion of a new doublet i.e. cutting out in his imagination the style of a new upper body garment.

turned orthography i.e. become pompous in his use of words.

fantastical banquet i.e. feast for the imagination. Benedick continues the image.

converted i.e. fall in love.

love may . . . an oyster i.e. love may make me a passive creature.

one woman shall not come in my grace i.e. one woman will not find favour with me – quibbling on the previous meaning of grace – virtue.

I'll none i.e. I'll have nothing to do with her.

cheapen Bid for.

noble (a) of high moral qualities (b) a gold coin.

angel (a) divine spirit (b) an even more valuable gold coin, two angels being equivalent to the three nobles above.

Monsieur Love Claudio.

arbour Shady, tree-covered retreat.

fit the kid-fox with a pennyworth i.e. see that this fox-cub gets what he deserves.

tax Order.

slander Do injustice to.

witness Evidence.

put . . . perfection i.e. be modest.

woo Beg.

in notes i.e. with music.

crotchets (a) in music a short note, half the value of a minim (b) odd, irrelevant ideas.

nothing Probably pronounced 'noting', hence strengthening the punning sequence.

Now . . . ravished Benedick is anticipating satirically what he imagines the next comments will be.

sheep's guts Used for instrument strings.

hale Haul.

horn i.e. a manly, hunting instrument.

Hey nonny, nonny i.e. into happiness.

ditties Short, simple songs.

dumps Depressions, low spirits.

shift (a) change (b) device (here for influencing Benedick).

bode no mischief Foretold no misfortune.

as lief As soon.

night-raven In folklore, a nocturnal bird whose cry foretold disaster.

what plague What calamity.

Stalk on A hunting metaphor meaning 'go on carefully towards the game'.

fowl i.e. Benedick.

Sits the wind . . . corner? Is that the way the wind blows – is that how things are?

enraged affection i.e. maddened love.

the infinite of thought Beyond the imagination.

counterfeit Pretend.

like enough Quite likely.

life of passion Real life.

discovers Reveals.

invincible Impregnable.

a gull A hoax or trick.

Knavery Wickedness.

ta'en the infection . . . up i.e. we have got him; keep it up.

smock Undergarment (particularly used as a nightgown).

between the sheet Pun involving sexual innuendo (a) written on the same sheet (b) in bed together.

halfpence A small coin, hence here torn into many small pieces.

railed at Abused.

ecstasy Frenzy.

overborne Overcome.

by some other From someone else.

An he should . . . hang him If he should, it would be charitable to hang him.

blood Passion.

proofs Examples.

dotage Foolish love.

daffed . . . respects Put aside all other considerations.

made her half myself i.e. my equal, by marrying her.

bate Reduce.

tender Offer.

contemptible Contemptuous.

proper Admirable.

outward happiness Well-favoured outward appearance.

in my mind As I think.

Hector One of the bravest of the Trojans, killed during the Greek siege of Troy.

howsoever Even if.

large jests Rather too free actions.

wear it out with good counsel Get over it with good advice.

net i.e. trap, but another metaphor from hunting.

sport will be Fun will come.

hold one an opinion Each think that the (other).

no such matter There's nothing to support it.

dumb-show Prelude. A mimed summary formerly preceded the play itself.

sadly borne Seriously carried out.

have their full bent Are stretched to the limit. A metaphor from archery – when the bow is fully flexed.

requited Returned.

proudly Contemptuously.
detractions Deficiencies, things that spoil reputations.
put them to mending i.e. make them good.
reprove Disprove, contradict.
horribly Completely.
quirks Quips, sharp verbal remarks.
broken on me i.e. used against me.
sentences Pointed sayings.
paper bullets Harmless missiles (because verbal).
awe Deter.
career of his humour Course of his inclination.
pains Trouble.
daw Jackdaw.
withal With.
Jew Unchristian, hence uncharitable.

Revision questions on Act II

1 Write a character sketch of Claudio as he appears in this Act.
2 How far is the theme of deception important to our appreciation of Act II?
3 Write an essay on the use of word-play in Act II.
4 Which do you find the most dramatically effective scene in Act II? Give reasons for your answer.

Act III Scene 1

Hero plans the deception of Beatrice. Margaret is sent to tell her that Hero and Ursula are talking about her in the garden. Beatrice goes to the garden and overhears the conspirators discussing that Benedick is sick with love for Beatrice. He has not revealed this to Beatrice and the conspirators decide – or appear to decide – that despite all Benedick's virtues Beatrice must not be told of his love. Beatrice decides that she will try to respond favourably to Benedick's love in the future.

Commentary

This scene, though in verse, parallels the previous one, employing the same devices and consonant imagery. Hero's verse is elevated; note the comparison in her opening speech between the growing and overarching honeysuckle and the favourites of princes – an oblique reference to the structure of the play itself.

This is ironic since Hero is unconscious of the application. Just as Don Pedro had noted the hidden Benedick in the previous scene, so here Hero notes 'For look where Beatrice, like a lap-wing, runs/Close by the ground to hear our conference.' Again, the parallel with nature reinforces the deception, which is unnatural; it does not end here, since the bringing together of two people admirably balanced – Benedick and Beatrice – is in some ways a natural act. Beatrice, like Benedick, is fish for the bait, and has to hear herself pronounced as being incapable of love or of making 'sport' of Benedick's love for her. The praise of Benedick is fulsome, with appropriate imagery, but Hero utters a sentiment which is to apply ironically to herself when they speak of Beatrice as being 'limed':

If it prove so, then loving goes by haps;
Some Cupid kills with arrows, some with traps.

Beatrice, like Benedick previously, responds with love for love; her ecstasy takes the form of a ten-line verse, almost a short sonnet. The concluding couplet – used in the Elizabethan form of the sonnet employed by Shakespeare – effectively ends the scene. Beatrice reveals a capacity for rhetoric which conveys, by the movement of the lines, her passion, but there is moving poetry in it too when she speaks of 'Taming my wild heart to thy loving hand.'

Proposing Discussing.
like favourites ... bred it See the commentary above, but the general meaning appears to be that those raised by princes often turn against them and deceive them – a not inappropriate comparison since deception is the theme of much of the play.
office Task.
trace Tread.
like a lapwing An unflattering comparison. The lapwing is the plover, a woodland bird that runs crouching, with wings spread low over the ground.
conference Discussion.
couched Concealed.
woodbine coverture Honeysuckle covered bower.
haggards Untrained hawks.
new-trothed i.e. Claudio, to whom I have just become engaged.
affection i.e. his love.
as full as fortunate i.e. as good a wife as Beatrice would be.
couch lie.
As much as may be yielded to a man i.e. Beatrice's virginity, her body.
  The speech, however, reminds us that Hero is soon to yield her body

to Claudio, though not before she is suspected of yielding herself to another lover.

fram'd Made.

Misprising Undervaluing.

shape . . . project Appearance . . . idea.

self-endeared Fond of herself.

rarely featured Handsome, distinguished looking.

spell him backward Turn everything he said to an unfavourable meaning. Spell is (a) utter, tell and (b) bewitch by a magic formula.

be her sister i.e. look effeminate.

black Dark-complexioned.

drawing of an antic i.e. like a caricature or clown.

ill-headed i.e. without a proper point.

agate very vilely cut Very badly shaped dwarf.

vane Weather-vane (influenced by everything).

block Stone.

simpleness . . . purchaseth Simple honesty . . . deserves.

carping Fault-finding.

from all fashions Contrary to all standards.

cover'd fire Damped down, but continuing to burn.

die with tickling Presumably being 'tickled to death' with laughter.

honest slanders Note the paradox, since 'slanders' are false.

stain Slander.

empoison Poison.

priz'd Reckoned.

only man i.e. greatest.

fancy Mind, whim.

argument Conversation.

When are you married When will you be married?

attires This probably means 'head-dresses'.

furnish me Supply what I need.

lim'd Caught with bird-lime, a sticky substance.

haps Chance incidents.

fire . . . ears i.e. they are 'burning' with what she has heard.

maiden pride i.e. in being a virgin.

such i.e. such faults as contempt and pride.

Taming . . . hand A hawking metaphor, perhaps more suitable as a bird image for Beatrice than the 'lapwing' comparison.

holy band Marriage.

reportingly i.e. than by mere report.

Act III Scene 2

Benedick, greatly changed in mood, shows all the symptoms of love, and is mocked by Don Pedro, Leonato and Claudio. Don John enters with his rehearsed news of Hero's unfaithfulness, offering to demonstrate it by inviting them to observe her window at midnight. Claudio asserts that if he finds that Hero is guilty, he will shame her in the church the following day.

Commentary

The focus is on the change in Benedick, with an inherent mockery of this his latest affectation. The word-play now is at the expense of Benedick, sharp and thrusting as his own at the expense of others in the past. There is a particularly effective running wit about the new care he is taking over his appearance. The irony encompasses the fact that just as Don Pedro and Claudio are exulting over their plot – already strengthened by that of Hero and Margaret and Ursula – Don John's plot against Claudio is implemented by the appearance of that genuinely melancholy man. Don John reveals his cunning again by making sure that Claudio remains for his 'revelations' about Hero. Claudio's reactions are immediate and despicable – he does not pause to think, and nor does Don Pedro – that the man retailing this gossip was proved to be a liar in Act II Scene 1. Notice that the supposed dark deeds – and the dark deeds of Don John – are to be proven at night, a kind of symbolic underlining of the black comedy which is woven into the play in the persons of Don John, Borachio and Conrade.

consummate i.e. consummated by the act of sexual intercourse.
vouchsafe Graciously permit.
bold with i.e. bold enough to ask.
little hangman i.e. rascal (here used playfully).
Gallants i.e. gentlemen, friends.
truant Idle rogue.
wants Lacks.
Draw it . . . Hang it! The punishment for traitors was to be hung, drawn and quartered; this is therefore witty, improvised punning.
a humour or a worm Toothache was believed to be caused either by the damp or a worm which ate into the tooth. One name for toothache was in fact 'the worm'.
fancy . . . fancy (a) love (b) inclination.
slops Loose-fitting breeches.
doublet Spanish cloak.
old signs i.e. the habitual signs (of being in love).
old ornament . . . cheek i.e. his beard. (Beatrice had expressed a dislike of beards, hence Benedick's action.)
Nay Here the word is not used contradictorily, but as an introduction to a more positive statement than the previous one.
civet Strong, musky perfume.

paint himself Use make-up.

crept into a lute-string Love-songs were usually accompanied by the lute, hence this is another jibe at Benedick's new practices.

governed by stops (a) controlled by the fret or stops on the neck of the lute (b) characterized by stops and starts.

heavy Tedious.

ill conditions Bad qualities.

buried with her face upwards i.e. under the body of her lover.

charm Magic spell (here for curing).

hobby-horses Buffoons.

For my life This is a wild oath or wager.

break with Disclose to.

Margaret Almost certainly 'Ursula' should be named here for consistency.

the two bears Beatrice and Benedick, who are both verbally 'savage'.

Good den Good evening.

If your leisure served If you are not busy.

aim better at me i.e. see me more clearly. A metaphor from archery.

manifest Reveal.

suit ill spent i.e. wasted courtship.

circumstances shortened To get down to essential details.

she . . . a talking of i.e. we have been speaking of her too long.

disloyal Unfaithful.

Leonato's Hero Note the bitterness of this, which plays on family and sexual belonging, in the latter case promiscuity.

paint out Depict, define.

worse title Infamous name.

Wonder not till further warrant Do not be amazed or doubtful before you have seen other evidence.

proceed accordingly Act as you wish.

disparage Dishonour.

coldly Calmly.

untowardly turned i.e. which has turned out adversely.

thwarting Obstructing.

plague i.e. disease, dishonour.

sequel After-consequence.

Act III Scene 3

Dogberry, the master-constable, and Verges, his assistant, are briefing their night-watchmen on their duties. Some time later, Borachio's boastful account of the successful execution of Don John's treacherous plan is overheard by the Watch who are sitting on 'the church-bench'. Although it is doubtful if the watchmen actually understand what they have overheard, they arrest the conspirators.

Commentary

Dogberry's combination of self-importance, misinformation and ignorance provide light relief. Notice that the word-play here takes the form largely of malapropisms, words used incorrectly because they sound like the correct word (as in the first one where 'salvation' is used for 'starvation'). There is a certain humour in the choice of names (like Dogberry and Seacoal, for example), and there is a particular Englishness about the Watch which contrasts with the actual Messina scene. The contrast too is emphasized by the colloquial nature of the prose, but stuctural unity is provided by the fact that once again what is *overheard* is important. Most of the exchanges between the Watch are ridiculous and bumbling, a further contrast with the contrived machinations of Don John. Again there is dual interaction, as there has been in the 'overhearing' scenes involving Benedick and Beatrice separately, with the overhearers and the overheard commanding the double attention of the audience. As Borachio recounts the success of the plot, he and Conrade are arrested by those who cannot understand it – a fine ironic and dramatic stroke.

compartner Companion and partner.
salvation Presumed malapropism for 'starvation'.
watch Town guard at night.
charge Instruction on their duties.
desartless Literally 'without merit', here 'deserving'.
well-favoured Good-looking.
comes by nature i.e. is an inherited gift, but there is a play on 'nature' or 'natural', meaning 'simple'.
favour Appearance.
no need Need – typical of Dogberry to get it the wrong way round.
senseless Sensible.
constable Sergeant.
bear Carry.
comprehend Apprehend.
vagrom Vagrant.
meddle Mix.
tolerable Intolerable.
endured Permitted.
belongs to Goes with being.
ancient i.e. old hand, also a senior member of the inns of court, an elderly lawyer.
quiet Hardly appropriate to a watchman, who might be expected to make a noise if anything is wrong.
bills Long handled weapons with pikes or blades at the end.

let them alone Note that Dogberry has no real idea of the Watch's function.

Well Right.

true Honest.

make Have to do.

more Better.

they that touch pitch will be defiled A biblical proverb (Ecclesiasticus, 13,1) meaning those that touch dirt will themselves be made dirty.

peaceable Peaceful.

steal Go quietly away (with a pun of course on 'steal').

still Quieten.

present Represent.

stay Stop.

statutes Laws (which Dogberry domonstrates that he doesn't know by inventing the offence to 'stay' a man against his will).

without Unless.

chances Occurs.

keep . . . your own A corruption of the instruction to a jury before a trial.

coil Fuss, part of the 'ado' of the play's title.

vigitant Vigilant.

Mass An oath 'By the mass'.

my elbow itched i.e. I thought that there was someone behind me.

scab (a) skin disease – the itch, with a crust forming over the sore (b) scoundrel.

owe thee Repay you later with.

penthouse Overhanging roof.

true drunkard A reference to Borachio's name and to the proverbial idea that the truth is revealed unconsciously by a drunkard.

close Hidden.

make what price Negotiate what terms.

unconfirmed Inexperienced.

nothing to a man No connection with the man who wears it.

deformed Disfiguring.

goes up and down i.e. parades about, behaves like.

vane The weather-vane.

how giddily a turns about (a) fashion, changes of style (b) the movement of the weather-vane.

hot bloods Excitable and fashionable young men.

fashioning Causing them to dress.

Pharaoh's soldiers Probably a reference to the painting (Exodus, 14, 23-8) of Pharaoh's men drowning in the Red Sea whilst in pursuit of Moses.

reechy Smoke-blackened.

Bel's Belonging to Baal, the God of the Canaanites in the Old Testament.

smirched Dirty.

codpiece Bag-shaped flap on the front of men's breeches, corresponding to the flies or zip on trousers.

massy Bulky, with obvious sexual innuendo.

giddy Dizzy.

shifted Moved, with a pun on 'shift' meaning 'loose undergarment' and perhaps 'change of wind'.

vilely Badly, but it is a 'bad' tale anyway.

possessed Put in possession of the facts.

possessed Took possession of.

appointed Supposed to do.

o'er-night The preceding evening.

recovered i.e. discovered.

lechery Most likely a malapropism for 'treachery'.

commonwealth Messina was clearly not a commonwealth, but the word sounds important.

lock Love-lock, a lock of hair separated from the rest and often decorated.

obey Malapropism for 'oblige'.

commodity (a) consignment (b) convenience (used ironically).

bills (a) weapons (see earlier notes in this scene) (b) inventory of goods in a consignment (c) instructions on payment in exchange for a consignment.

in question (a) to be questioned (b) under interrogation.

Act III Scene 4

Hero, Margaret and Ursula are discussing what Hero should wear for her wedding, though Hero is out of spirits. When Beatrice arrives she too is depressed, but Margaret is full of taunting remarks which carry sexual innuendoes. She compares the change in Benedick with that in Beatrice who, devoid of her customary wit, can only respond irritably as 'all the gallants of the town' arrive to escort Hero to church.

Commentary

There is a sense of foreboding in Hero's heaviness of heart, though Margaret's composure and free wit suggest that she is unaware of the significance of the previous night's scene at Hero's window. Margaret's wit constrasts effectively with the mood of Hero and Beatrice, and there is dramatic tension in the fact that nothing has been revealed, so that the audience awaits the imminent denunciation of Hero. The deception of Beatrice continues, and her melancholy may be contrasted with that of Benedick in Scene 2 of this act. Margaret's witty verve usurps Beatrice's own wit. She teases her about Benedick.

rebato Type of ruff.

tire Head-dress.

hair Triming of false hair.

thought Trifle, very small amount.

exceeds Excels.

night-gown Dressing-gown. The description that follows scarcely supports this disparaging term.

respect of Comparison with.

cuts i.e. slashes in a garment made to expose material of a different colour.

down-sleeves Enclosed sleeves from shoulder to wrist.

side-sleeves Open sleeves hanging from the shoulder.

round underborne Supported all round from below.

tinsel Cloth interwoven with gold or silver thread.

quaint Fashionable.

on't Of it.

Fie upon thee . . . ashamed? You ought to be ashamed! (A remark which underlines Hero's innocence.)

saving your reverence i.e. excuse me for mentioning the word.

And bad thinking . . . speaking i.e. if bad thinking doesn't twist the meaning of honesty.

light Unchaste.

sick tune Miserable frame of mind.

all other tune i.e. I'm not fit for anything.

Clap's Let us strike up.

'Light o' Love' A popular song at the time.

without a burden (a) lightly, gaily (b) with no part for a bass (c) with no chorus or refrain.

Ye . . . with your heels! An insulting remark meaning that Margaret is wanton, always ready for love-making. We see how changed Beatrice is – normally she would have delighted in this.

stables . . . barns Buildings for domestic animals, with barns being places for storing crops but also a pun on 'bairns' – children.

illegitimate construction Illogical interpretation, with perhaps a pun on 'bastard children'.

scorn . . . heels Spurn, with a reference back to Beatrice's remark.

heigh-ho! A weary sigh, but perhaps, in view of Margaret's question, a cry used in hawking, in riding, or even a domestic response.

H A quibble on 'ache' which was then pronounced 'aitch'.

be not turned Turk i.e. if you haven't abandoned your vows of celibacy.

sailing by the star i.e. the Pole star. The implication is that nothing could be relied on any more.

trow? Do you think?

gloves A traditional wedding present, often perfumed.

stuffed (a) with a blocked nose (b) pregnant.

apprehension Learning.

you left it i.e. took leave of your senses.

enough Punning on 'rarely'.
carduus benedictus This is a medicinal herb, the Holy Thistle, with a
  convenient pun on Benedick's name.
qualm Sudden feeling of sickness.
prick'st Hero also indulges a little sexual innuendo.
list Like.
eats his meat without grudging Accepts his lot in life without
  complaint.
false gallop Literally 'canter' – Margaret is still boasting of the speed of
  her replies.

Act III Scene 5

Dogberry and Verges long-windedly advise Leonato that they
are holding two villains for questioning. The old man, on the
way to his daughter's wedding and already pressed for time,
authorizes them to conduct the examination themselves.

Commentary

This scene is rich in dramatic irony. The wordiness of Dogberry
and Verges acts as a dramatically effective delaying tactic – the
audience is on edge to know what will happen. At the same time
the audience knows that the 'arrant knaves' have been caught
and suspects that Hero's name will ultimately be cleared – unless
of course the muddle-headedness and incompetence of Dogberry and Verges lets them escape.

confidence Conference (continuing the sequence of malapropisms
  begun in Scene 2).
decerns Concerns.
Goodman A complimentary prefix.
off the matter i.e. digresses.
honest as the skin between his brows Eyebrows having no skin
  between them – in other words, which meet – were thought to betoken
  dishonesty.
odorous Odious.
palabras Spanish for 'words', probably indicating to Verges that he
  should mind what he says.
to bestow it all on your worship i.e. to give him all his tediousness to
  Leonato – unconscious irony, since Dogberry thinks that he is being
  flattering.
exclamation Acclamation (praise).
fain Like to.
excepting your worship's presence By your leave, with your
  permission.

arrant Notorious.

age is in, wit is out i.e. when you get old you lose your senses.

a world to see i.e. what a world this is.

as ever broke bread i.e. as ever ate.

he comes too short of you i.e. he gets to the point quicker than you do.

comprehended Apprehended.

aspicious Suspicious.

suffigance Sufficient.

Francis Almost certainly he means 'George' – a minor error on Shakespeare's part.

examination Examine.

spare for no wit i.e. lack no insight.

non-come A malapropism for *non compos mentis* – not in one's right mind.

excommunication This is the best of the malapropisms so far, a combination of 'examination' and 'communication'.

Revision questions on Act III

1 Compare and contrast the traps laid for Beatrice and Benedick, as well as the reactions of each character to being 'loved'.

2 Indicate the nature of the comedy, giving some detail, in the actions of Dogberry and the Watch.

3 In what ways is dramatic tension aroused in Act III?

4 What aspects of Act III constitute 'black' comedy?

5 Write a short character sketch of either Margaret *or* Leonato *or* Dogberry *or* Hero as she/he appears in this Act.

Act IV Scene 1

In the church, Claudio delivers his strongly worded melodramatic denunciation of Hero and includes Leonato in his accusation. Hero denies the charges, but is stunned by the shock and swoons. Don Pedro supports Claudio by saying that he witnessed what happened. Leonato feels that death is the best way out for Hero. When the accusers leave, the Friar, Beatrice and Benedick attempt to revive Hero. Beatrice reveals that she had not slept with Hero the previous night as was her usual practice. The Friar now tries to pacify a distraught Leonato; he is convinced of her innocence, and certain that there has been a terrible misunderstanding. Benedick assumes that this must be the work of Don John. The Friar evolves a plan in which a report is put about that Hero has died; pity and remorse will then force Claudio to see things differently and regret his behaviour. Benedick adds his support and Leonato is won round. When the others have gone, Beatrice and Benedick confess their love for each other, and Beatrice persuades a reluctant Benedick to challenge Claudio to a duel.

Commentary

There is a superb dramatic opening to this scene with Claudio's denial that he comes to 'marry' Hero, the seriousness of this lost initially in a play on words. The unequivocal nature of Claudio's language – he calls Hero 'this rotten orange' – underlines the sick nature of the comedy which here seems to be on the dramatic edge of tragedy. Ironically, Claudio stresses the appearance and reality nature of Hero's 'deception', not realizing that he himself is the victim of it. The language – 'the heat of a luxurious bed' – is dangerously near the language of tragedy in, for example, *Hamlet* and *Othello*.

At first we feel the pathos of Leonato's situation, though Claudio's profession of 'brotherly' treatment of Hero has a cloying effect and Hero's own innocence is the central focus of this part of the scene. This is enhanced by the misguided support of Don Pedro for Claudio's accusations, and the cunningly weighted if brief interjections of Don John. Throughout Claudio sets much store by 'honour', to him and his kind a quality of paramount importance. Claudio's rhetoric carries him into a kind of melodramatic parody of the word-play in the play, while Leonato feels keenly his own loss of 'honour' rather than feeling for the suffering of his daughter. In fact Leonato's own outburst, which echoes Claudio's, partakes of the same sick selfishness, while the apparent confirmation of Hero's guilt through the fact that Beatrice was not 'her bedfellow' adds to the dramatic tension.

The role of the Friar now becomes crucial, but Benedick reveals his own insight – there is no acting with words here – that Don John is the root cause of the deception of Claudio and Don Pedro. Yet deception remains the main theme, for the Friar's deception, his plan to proclaim Hero dead, is in the cause of good, with repentance as the outcome. (The interested student will note the same theme in *The Winter's Tale* where Hermione, proclaimed dead after the false accusations of her madly jealous husband Leontes, survives in secret and is produced in the form of a statue to receive her husband's repentance and love.) Again Benedick's voice is strong in acceptance of the plan.

The major effects of the scene are admirably contrasted with the reactions of Beatrice and Benedick when they are left alone. In brief, they surface from word-play to an unequivocal confession of their love for each other; it is moving, poignant in its simplicity, but climaxed by Beatrice's direct injunction to Benedick 'Kill Claudio.' Her spirited defence of Hero, her superb command of extreme (not melodramatic) language, completely overcomes Benedick, who can hardly get a word in. He reluctantly agrees to fight Claudio; it is a measure of his love and, perhaps indeed of his integrity.

No Note the immediate dramatic impact of this single word.
conjoined Joined together.
what men dare do! Claudio is here indulging his bitterness, with the corollary of what women do – i.e. Hero.
Interjections? Exclamations, with a play on parts of speech.
of laughing i.e. funny; Benedict goes on to give simple interjections.
by your leave With your permission (but Claudio is being overly polite in view of what he is about to reveal).
unconstrained i.e. without any doubts or qualifications.
counterpoise Balance.
render Hand back.
learn Teach.
thankfulness Gratitude.
rotten orange i.e. the fact that the orange was rotten would not be noticed until the peel was removed, with the implication that Hero's 'peel' – her outer covering of innocence – has been exposed by the previous night's scene.
honour The key word, as far as Claudio is concerned.
authority Testimony.
cover Conceal.
Comes not that blood i.e. Hero's blushes.
luxurious Lecherous.
approved wanton Proven woman of loose morals.
in your own proof To find out for yourself.
vanquish'd . . . youth Taken advantage of her inexperience.
made defeat Broken.
'forehand Aforementioned.
word too large i.e. persuaded her to let me make love to her.
comely Proper.
Out on thee Away with you.
seeming Apparent, though perhaps deceptive. Hero's 'seemed' meant simply 'appeared'.
write against Disparage.
Dian in her orb Diana, the moon-goddess in Roman mythology, patroness of virgins.
ere it be blown Before it blooms.

intemperate Excessively indulgent (licentious).

blood Passion.

Venus Roman goddess of love, especially sensual love.

wide i.e. wide of the mark.

stale Prostitute.

move Put.

kindly Natural.

have in her Have over her (influence).

beset Surround by hostility.

catechizing Questioning.

your name i.e. what you are.

that can Hero Hero can do that.

itself Note the deliberate de-personalizing of Hero since in Claudio's eyes she is guilty.

grieved Aggrieved.

liberal Loose-living.

There is not chastity . . . them Don John implies that language itself will be made indecent by the repetition of Hero's unfaithfulness.

much misgovernment Sexual misbehaviour.

half . . . heart i.e. your inner self was half as good as your outer.

foul . . . fair Note that the words, as in *Macbeth*, strike the idea of appearance and reality. In fact it is Claudio's reactions which are most foul, Hero's innocence which is most fair.

pure impiety and impious purity Unrelieved wickedness and wicked though appearing innocent.

For thee I'll lock up Because of you I renounce love.

on my eyelids shall conjecture hang i.e. I shall look at everything suspiciously.

thoughts of harm i.e. capable of wounding.

Smother her spirits up i.e. overcome her.

blood Blushes.

on the rearward of Following.

but one Only one child.

Chid Rebuked.

frugal Nature's frame i.e. because Nature only allowed me one child.

one too much One more than was enough.

issue Child.

moving-delicate Touching the feelings with their charms.

liver In Elizabethan times the liver was thought to be the seat of love and passion.

fashion the event So bring about the outcome.

lay it down in likelihood Set down as being likely.

quench the wonder of her infamy i.e. overcome public astonishment at her unfaithfulness.

sort not Does not turn out.

reclusive Secluded.

inwardness Intimacy.

justly Rightly.

your soul your body i.e. with complete integrity.

flow (a) melt (b) am crying.

twine Thread.

For to strange sores . . . strain the cure i.e. for unconventional problems you need unconventional answers.

die to live i.e. pretend to die now in order to have a good life in the future (note the word-play even by the Friar).

prolong'd Postponed.

even Straightforward.

Do not swear and eat it Do not swear and then have to eat your words.

mir'd Muddied.

infamy Disgrace.

That I myself . . . Valuing of her i.e. I valued her more than I valued myself.

season Seasoning i.e. to hide her disgrace.

attir'd Overwhelmed by.

belied Slandered.

barr'd up . . . ribs of iron i.e. already a cast-iron case against you.

given way unto this course of fortune Let events take their course.

noting Observing.

apparitions Reactions.

innocent shames i.e. shame because of the accusations of which she is innocent.

angel whiteness Deathly pallor.

burn the errors i.e. as if they were heretics at the stake.

her maiden truth i.e. virgin innocence.

reading i.e. of her face.

experimental seal Confirmation of experience.

tenor of my book Substance of my speech.

proper nakedness Rightly appears for all to see.

unmeet Improper.

Maintain'd the change i.e. held an intimate conversation with.

misprision Mistake.

the very bent Every indication.

practice Treachery.

frame Action of destruction.

dried i.e. drained of emotion or life.

invention Ability to scheme.

havoc of my means Chaos of my resources.

reft Deprived.

kind Manner.

policy Shrewdness.

monument Tomb.

rites Formal practices.

carried Managed.

travail Labour, especially connected with childbirth.

greater birth i.e. a more important outcome.

to the worth Up to its true value.

lack'd Seen to be missing.

rack Stretch out beyond the normal.

The virtue that possession . . . ours i.e. its real value when we had it (but did not know we had it).

study of imagination i.e. into his mind imaginatively as he thinks about it.

organ Faculty.

apparell'd in more precious habit To appear all the more precious.

by it i.e. by the sword.

devised to Created for.

protest Declare.

stayed Stopped.

in a happy hour i.e. at a lucky time.

Tarry Wait.

I am gone i.e. you have lost me.

approved in the height Undeniably to the utmost degree.

bear her in hand Lead her on.

take hands i.e. in marriage.

uncovered Unearthed.

unmitigated rancour Complete bitterness.

eat his heart in the market-place Note the strength of these sentiments which emphasize Beatrice's loyalty to Hero and her anger on Hero's behalf.

A proper saying! What a fine thing to say!

undone Ruined (by false words).

princely testimony (a) evidence of his princely nature (b) evidence that a prince would give.

goodly count (a) fine allegation (b) likely story (c) splendid nobleman.

Comfect Confection, sweet.

melted into curtsies i.e. softened into servile courtesies or courtly behaviour (a continuation of the derogatory 'sweet' metaphor).

valour into compliment Bravery into a ceremonial act of courtesy.

only turned into tongue Become only talkers.

By this hand i.e. his own.

engaged Pledged, won over to your cause.

By this hand i.e. Beatrice's.

render me . . . account Answer to me dearly for his conduct.

As you hear of me . . . me i.e. trust me to act as I know you would wish me to act.

Act IV Scene 2

The examination of Borachio and Conrade is conducted by Dogberry. In spite of the master constable's total ineptitude before the sexton, the facts of the conspiracy emerge largely due to the intervention of the sexton in the questioning. The sexton realizes the importance of the information, for he has already heard how Hero has been rejected and died, and gives orders that the conspirators should be bound and taken before the governor Leonato.

Commentary

Contrast is of the essence here, since this scene follows immediately upon the church denunciation scene; there words were weapons, here words are the bumbling expressions of incompetence which yet manages to defeat villainy. Here deception is exposed; in the previous scene what was *thought it to be* deception was condemned. The nature of the comedy here springs from the malapropisms and the time taken to get everything done, the scene once more rousing dramatic expectation through the simple device of delay. Of further dramatic interest is the gradual revelation of the conspiracy and Don John's implication in it. The latter has thought fit to leave Messina, a sure underlining of guilt, and an undermining of the confidence of Borachio and Conrade. Dogberry demonstrates an incredible pomposity and an uncomprehending verbosity; we note how his word miss-play balances the subtle word-play of Beatrice and Benedick elsewhere in *Much Ado About Nothing*.

gowns Robes of office.
dissembly Assembly.
that I am . . . partner Typical of Dogberry's self-importance. He affects to understand the word 'malefactors' and claims the title for himself and Verges, not realizing that its meaning is 'criminals'.
exhibition Commission.
sirrah Fellow (spoken contemptuously).
defend Forbid.
go near to be On the point of being.
we are none i.e. we are not knaves.
go about with Turn the tables on.
'Fore God A sacrilegious oath 'Swear before God'.
they are both in a tale They are both telling the same story.
Prince John a villain Note that ironically this is true, though at this stage thought 'perjury' by Dogberry.
flat perjury Dogberry means 'downright slander'.
burglary It's difficult to know what this is a malapropism for – it seems to merely reinforce the idea of 'slander'.
by mass An everyday oath.
upon his words On the basis of what he said.

redemption Perdition.
refused Denied.
before Ahead.
opinionated Pinioned – having their arms bound.
coxcomb Clown.
God's my life An oath 'May God save my life'.
naughty varlet Worthless rogue.
suspect my place Respect my position.
that I am an ass Dogberry's repetition of the word 'ass' and his obvious
  misunderstanding of it greatly contributes to the verbal comedy.
piety Impiety.
as pretty a piece of flesh Dogberry is not exactly modest.
to go Away with you.
had losses i.e. life has not been without its problems (largely financial
  ones). This may even be a reference to his previous status.
two gowns Since these were costly, it reinforces the idea that Dogberry
  was once rich (or is boasting that he was).

Revision questions on Act IV

1 In what ways is Claudio's denunciation of Hero in church
typical of the 'black' comedy of *Much Ado About Nothing*?
2 What changes have occurred in Beatrice and Benedick since
the beginning of the play? You should refer closely to the text in
your answer.
3 Give the reactions of (a) Don Pedro (b) Leonato and (c) the
Friar during and after the church scene.
4 Indicate the part played by (a) Dogberry and (b) the Sexton in
Act IV Scene 2.

Act V Scene 1

Leonato rejects his brother's attempts to advise him, and when
Claudio and the Prince, Don Pedro, come to take their leave,
Leonato accuses them of slander and murder. He challenges
Claudio to a duel, but this challenge is not accepted. Antonio
takes up the challenge on his brother's behalf and intensifies the
verbal provocation to such an extent that Leonato is obliged to
take him away. Claudio and Don Pedro are joined by Benedick,
to whom they look for light relief after the previous exchanges,
but Benedick is angry and, brushing aside their jokes, challenges
Claudio to a duel. This time the challenge is accepted. Dogberry,
Verges and the watch bring in the bound conspirators. The
Prince fails to get an intelligible reply from Dogberry concerning the offence that has been committed, but Borachio confesses

everything. The sexton meanwhile brings in Leonato and his brother; the Prince and Claudio, embarrassed by their 'mistake', offer to do penance. Claudio's punishment is to marry Hero's cousin after a night of mourning for Hero. Borachio exonerates Margaret from any blame, but Leonato wishes to question her further.

Commentary

As befits something approaching tragedy, the first part of the scene in which Leonato indulges his grief is in elevated blank verse. There is a degree of pathos in this but it is the pathos of age since Leonato can be no match for Claudio. Nevertheless the language reflects his anger and raises the dramatic temperature of the scene. Leonato's anger, however, changes to concern when his brother Antonio, even less of a match for Claudio, challenges him in turn to a duel. Both challenges are a source of obvious embarrassment to Claudio and Don Pedro.

These two are condescending when they encounter Benedick, Claudio referring contemptuously to 'two old men without teeth'. The changed Benedick confuses them further; Claudio affects at first to laugh off the challenge (note the duplication of the challenge motif here) while Don Pedro further baits Benedick with Beatrice's supposed remarks about him in furtherance of their plot to bring Beatrice and Benedick together. In a superb summary of events – the fleeing of Don John and the 'death' of Hero – Benedick makes clear the seriousness of his challenge. We cannot help but wonder at the lack of feeling in Claudio in response to the news of Hero's 'death'. So intent are they on their own wit that Don Pedro and Claudio almost ignore the factual news that Don John has fled; by a fine dramatic stroke Dogberry and the Watch enter just at this moment.

Borachio's confession, superbly eloquent, straight (to contrast with his previous deception) is one of the high dramatic points of the scene. Claudio, honour satisfied, can now think of Hero as he did before, and we mark the shallowness of such a love which 'alters when it alteration finds' (to quote from Shakespeare's own Sonnet 116). Claudio does however agree to do penance (he is observing his own code of 'honour') though insisting that 'sinned I not/But in mistaking'. Plot contrivance is now firmly in Leonato's hands – he insists on repentance at Hero's tomb, though Claudio is quick to seize on the offer of the niece who is to be a substitute for Hero. Audience and reader must now suspend disbelief in this wholly unlikely necessity in order to round things off. Leonato's wish to interrogate Margaret indicates his determination to get to the bottom of the matter, while Dogberry continues to misconstrue and mis-utter (even calling Leonato 'a most thankful and reverend youth'). We must remember that we are watching a comedy and therefore should not place too high a premium on realism – the repentance and acceptance of Claudio and Don Pedro are essential to the working out of the happy ending.

second Reinforce.
overwhelm'd Turned upside down.
strain (a) extreme degree (b) pressure tending to alter shape.
thus for thus Like for like.
lineament Line.
stroke . . . beard Reflectively, like a philosopher.
wag Be off, depart.
Patch . . . proverbs Repair sorrow with wisdom or clever sayings.
candle-wasters Scholars, who read late at night.
yet Then.
gather Gain.
passion Pain or emotion.
give preceptial medicine Offer moral instruction or cure.
air Breath, talking.
office Custom.
wring Writhe.
sufficiency Capability.
The like i.e. the same thing.
advertisement (a) public advertisement by the town crier (b) advice given dictatorially.
in the style of gods i.e. in a manner above human suffering.
made a push at i.e. thrust at, as with a lance, taken on in combat.
bend Bind or aim (a metaphor from archery).
Are you so hasty now? Don Pedro has previously said that they would stay at least a month.
lie low i.e. be laid low.
dissembler Deceiver.
beshrew Curse.
meant nothing to Intended to do nothing with.
fleer Sneer.
dotard Senile old man.
being When I was.
to thy head To your face.
bruise i.e. scar.
trial of a man i.e. a duel.
fram'd Brought about.

prove it i.e. that what I say is true.

on his body By wounding him.

nice fence Carefully accurate style of fencing.

active practice Current practical experience.

lustihood State of vigorous strength.

men indeed Real men.

Win me and wear me i.e. beat me and wear me as a trophy.

boy . . . boy The repetition is intended to be particularly insulting.

whip you from Drive you off.

foining fence Fencing with the point, i.e. precisely, but it may mean 'foiling or frustrating defence' since Claudio will not take the challenge seriously.

Jacks Knaves.

milksops Effeminate men.

weigh Are valued at, worth.

utmost scruple The smallest weight, equal to about 1/24th of an ounce.

Scambling Gangling.

outfacing Brazen, acting defiantly.

fashion-monging Conforming to the latest fashion.

cog . . . flout Cheat . . . mock.

deprave Dishonour.

anticly Grotesquely.

durst Dare.

wake Excite, stir up.

smart Suffer.

like to have Almost.

doubt Suspect.

high-proof Impenetrable. A metaphor from armoury.

beaten away i.e. as an armourer beats metal.

wit . . . scabbard Benedick is indicating that he will let his sword do his talking, equivalent to the modern colloquial expression of 'put your money where your mouth is'.

Never any No one ever.

beside their wit Out of their minds.

as . . . minstrels i.e. by asking them to play, drawing the instrument from its case or drawing the bow across the instrument.

care killed a cat A proverbial expression meaning that a worried state of mind is destructive.

mettle Courage.

in the career The area enclosed for tilting at a tournament.

broke cross i.e. broken across. The point did not strike squarely.

By this light A mild oath expressing surprise.

turn his girdle i.e. (he) knows what to do if he wishes to fight. Wrestlers used to turn the buckles of their belts to the back when they were ready to fight.

make it good Substantiate my charge.

Do me right Give me satisfaction.

protest Publicly proclaim.

meet . . . good cheer . . . feast Note the sequence of puns, here on food, festivities, fighting.

bid Invited.

calf's head Daft, harmless person.

capon Castrated cockerel.

carve . . . curiously This implies that he will use his sword with great precision.

naught Worth nothing.

woodcock A game bird, thought to be particularly foolish because it was easily caught.

Just Just so, quite right.

a wise gentleman Implying an old man, full of cunning.

'hath the tongues' i.e. speaks foreign languages.

forswore Denied.

double tongue i.e. hypocrisy.

transshape Transform

the old man's daughter i.e. Hero. Note the distant use of Leonato since Hero's supposed faithfulnessness.

God saw him . . . garden This is an allusion to the story of Adam hiding in the garden of Eden, after disobeying God. They are hinting that Benedick hid in Leonato's garden and overheard what they said (Act II, Scene 2).

as braggarts do their blades i.e. as boastful men do, through incompetence, or to avoid real conflict through cowardice.

among you Between you.

Lord Lackbeard This is addressed to Claudio, and implies immaturity. Ironically, Benedick is now without his beard. (See Act III, Scene 2, 42-5).

meet i.e. in combat.

pretty Fine. This is ironically said.

leaves off his wit Loses his senses.

giant to an ape i.e. an even bigger fool.

doctor . . . man A scholar in comparison with him.

soft you Hush.

pluck up Pull yourself together.

sad Serious.

weigh more reasons in her balance i.e. judge cases again. There is also a pun on 'reasons' pronounced 'raisons' in the scales, or balance, of a shopkeeper.

and you be Since you are.

cursing hypocrite Freely swearing your innocence.

looked to Kept watch upon.

false report Told lies (in fact they have told the truth).

secondarily Secondly.

slanders Slanderers.

thirdly Notice that by getting the sequence deliberately wrong, Don Pedro is parodying Dogberry.

his own division i.e. differentiating in his own way.

suited Dressed up.

bound to your answer (a) obliged to reply to the charge against you (b) tied up as a result of what you have done.

cunning Clever (sarcastic).

answer (a) reply (b) retribution, punishment in return.

discover Reveal.

incensed Incited.

upon record Written down.

like iron i.e. like a weapon wounding you.

practice Performance, carrying out of.

compos'd and fram'd Made up and equipped.

rare semblance Fine appearance (as forecast by the Friar in Act IV, Scene 1, 223-5).

the plaintiffs Presumably Dogberry means 'the defendants'.

reformed Informed.

serve Provide the opportunity.

your wronger i.e. the one who has wronged you.

breath Speech, or merely being.

beliest Tell lies against.

honourable Leonato is being bitterly ironic, and by using 'honourable' turning Claudio's standards against himself.

Impose me to i.e. inflict on me.

invention Action of devising.

bend i.e. in submission.

enjoin me to Inflict on me.

bid you bid Ask you to ask – a kind of cynical pun.

Possess Put in possession of the facts.

labour Work out.

invention Composition.

yet Instead.

she alone is heir Leonato seems to have forgotten that Antonio has a son (1, 2, 1-2).

the right (a) to marry you (b) pun on 'rite' – marriage ceremony.

overkindness More kind than could be reasonably expected.

dispose Make over by way of a bargain.

naughty Wicked.

pack'd in A party to, an accomplice.

by her Of her.

under white and black i.e. black and white, in writing.

key A misunderstanding of Dogberry who has heard the word 'lock' and takes it to mean 'key'.

in God's name Beggars would ask for alms 'for God's sake'.

reverent youth Note the paradox.

There's i.e. money.

God save the foundation! The usual way of thanking for those who received alms at religious houses.

to correct yourself An unfortunate expression. He means 'correct him yourself'.
give Beg.
prohibit Grant.
lewd Good-for-nothing.

Act V Scene 2

Margaret spars suggestively with Benedick until she leaves to fetch Beatrice. The good-natured banter between Beatrice and Benedick is interrupted by the arrival of Ursula with the news that the conspiracy has been uncovered. She also summons Beatrice to Leonato's house, Benedick agreeing to go with her.

Commentary

This scene shows the progress of the love of Beatrice and Benedick, indicates once again the sharpness of their wit and Margaret's capacity for sexual innuendo. It also serves to act as a delaying scene before Claudio discovers the 'cousin's' true identity. Doubtless there is relief for Benedick in Ursula's news. But before that he has demonstrated that he cannot be the conventional lover by writing the requisite romantic poems to his mistress. He also reveals, with some pride, that he has challenged Claudio.

deserve well at my hands i.e. do me a favour that I shall be obliged to repay.
the speech of Talk to.
style (a) manner of writing (b) a pun on 'stile'.
come over (a) surpass, exceed (b) climb over.
comely Pleasing, attractive.
come over me i.e. have sexual intercourse with me.
below stairs i.e. remain a servant (and never have a man).
catches Captures, seizes.
foils Light swords with buttoned points.
give thee the bucklers i.e. acknowledge that I have no defence against you. Literally, hand over my shield.
swords . . . bucklers Potent sexual innuendo, 'swords' represent the penis and 'bucklers' the vagina.
pikes As above, though literally the spike is the centre of a buckler.
vice (a) a tool used to grip and hold a piece of work (b) bawdy pun for a 'woman's thighs'.
legs (a) the means of getting here (b) see 'vice' above – she can use her thighs sexually.

pitiful To be pitied.

deserve Am worthy.

Leander In mythology, he was drowned trying to swim across the Hellespont to see his beloved Hero.

Troilus Troilus was in love with Cressida, the niece of Pandarus. Shakespeare wrote a play, *Troilus and Cressida,* about their tragic love-story.

pandars Named after Pandarus (see above), the go-between.

quondam One-time, former.

carpet-mongers i.e. men famed for their living, rather than their fighting. A 'knight of the carpet' was one dubbed in time of peace, at court, as opposed to one dubbed on the field of battle.

the even road of a blank verse A carriage metaphor, implying that the writers of blank verse still used the same old heroes (and perhaps images), just as a carriage used well-beaten tracks.

turned over Completely bowled over.

'horn' . . . hard Sexual innuendo of male erection – Benedick is still thinking of being 'scorned' and 'cuckolded'.

born under a rhyming planet Suggesting that his lack of poetic ability is due to unfavourable astrological influences (compare this with Beatrice's 'a star danced').

festival Merry, in a holiday spirit.

'Then' i.e. her signal to depart.

that I came What I came for.

noisome Offensive, evil-smelling.

undergoes i.e. is under.

subscribe him Write him down as.

politic Skilfully arranged.

confession Remark.

instance Argument.

the time of good neighbours When men had no need to praise themselves, because their neighbours praised them.

monument Remembrance.

bell The funeral bell signifying his burial.

rheum Tears.

Don Worm . . . conscience Personification of the idea that the conscience eats away at a man's determination like a worm in the bud.

yonder's old coil There's a real fuss.

abused Deceived.

moreover, I will go with thee to thy uncle's Note the delicious sense of anti-climax after Benedick's romantic assertions.

Act V Scene 3

Claudio keeps his vigil by Hero's tomb. He hangs an epitaph there and has musicians sing a dirge, before leaving with Don Pedro for Leonato's house and the wedding ceremony.

Commentary

A ritualized scene, the dirge in rhyming lines resembling an incantation. The mood is sombre, as befits repentance, but there is a certain artificiality about it too which Don Pedro's heavier alternately rhyming lines seem to echo. This mood is picked up by Claudio presumably as a token of sincerity. Again knowing of the plot, we have to suspend our disbelief. The grief seems exaggerated even if the repentance is sincere.

of Leonato i.e. of his family.

Hero . . . here Note the near pun.

guerdon Reward for.

dumb Not here to speak for myself.

goddess of the night i.e. Diana, the moon-goddess, patroness of virgins.

virgin knight i.e. Hero (one of the followers of the goddess).

uttered Driven out.

wolves . . . prey'd i.e. the time of the night creatures is over.

wheels of Phoebus Chariot of the sun-god, also called Apollo.

other weeds Different clothes (for the wedding).

Hymen The Greek god of marriage.

luckier issue Happier outcome.

speed's i.e. help us to suceed.

qualify Explain.

largely In full.

let wonder seem familiar Treat the things you now find surprising as if they were commonplace.

Soft and fair i.e. gently.

no more than reason (a) no more than is reasonable (b) no more than I love reason.

friendly recompense i.e. returning affection.

halting sonnet Clumsy fourteen-line poem.

pure i.e. with nothing added by anyone else.

Fashion'd to Made for.

hands (a) handwritings (b) the actions of our own hands.

by this light An oath, originally referring to the sun.

by this good day An answering oath.

consumption i.e. wasting state.

Benedick . . . man See Act I, Scene 1, 247-8.

college of wit-crackers Collection of joke-makers.

flout Mock.

satire or an epigram The first is a lampoon or composition in which vices and follies are ridiculed, the second a short statement or poem with a witty ending.

beaten with brains Mentally defeated.

to any purpose Of any importance.

conclusion (a) judgment (b) end (c) final binding act.

Act V Scene 4

At Leonato's, Hero and Antonio are briefed on the parts they are to play at the wedding ceremony. Benedick requests the help of the Friar and the blessing of Leonato for his own marriage to Beatrice. Leonato cryptically confesses the part played by others in prompting this second marriage. Claudio accepts a masked woman to be his wife and the Friar promises a full explanation when she is revealed as Hero. Beatrice and Benedick find out that they have been the victims of deception, but when evidence of their genuine affection is produced, they agree to marry. Benedick will not allow the news that Don John has been recaptured to interfere with the dancing that ends the play.

Commentary

This is the last deception in a play which has had deception as its major theme. After that all masks – and this looks back to the mask *and* dancing scene of Act II – both real and metaphorical, are put away finally as all ends happily. The early exchanges stress innocence (with the exception of Margaret). Leonato's revelation that he and others are responsible for the plot to bring Beatrice and Benedick together does not dismay Benedick, who is now anxious to be married. Claudio's repentance and complete change of mood is shown in his agreeing to marry the 'niece' 'were she an Ethiope'. Benedick counters Claudio's jibes in rhyming verse. After a brisk exchange between Beatrice and Benedick where each denies loving the other but finally succumbs to acceptance, dancing and music bring about the end of the play, thus signifying harmony and a return to an orderly way of life.

against her will Unintentionally.
sort Turn out.
reckoning i.e. resolution, settlement.
confirm'd countenance Convincing appearance (i.e. straight face).
entreat your pains Beg to trouble you.
bind me (a) subject me to the bands of marriage (b) tie me up as a
   captive.
undo me Cause my downfall.
lent . . . gave i.e. it was Hero who caused Beatrice to regard Benedick
   'with an eye of favour'.

requite Repay.

from me ... Prince i.e. we caused you to look on Beatrice 'with an eye of love'.

May stand with ours i.e. your consent and good will in our marriage (that of himself and Beatrice).

Ethiope Literally Ethiopian, black woman.

February Wintry.

savage bull See Act I, 1, 241-2.

Europa (a) Europe the continent (b) the beauty carried off by Jove who was disguised as a bull.

amiable low Pleasant sound (i.e. the lowing of cattle).

leap'd Sprang upon in copulation.

your father's cow i.e. your mother.

got Begot.

bleat Derogatory, here meaning the bleat of a calf.

reck'nings Accounts to be dealt with.

kinsman Relative.

unbruised Uninjured.

cudgelled Beaten with a stick.

thy single life (a) the only life you have (b) your life as a bachelor.

double-dealer (a) married, as opposed to single (b) unfaithful.

look ... narrowly to Keep a close eye on.

lighten (a) lift the burden (b) put in a cheerful mood.

heels Benedick is looking forward both to dancing and to consummating the marriage.

staff (a) support (b) walking stick or the rod carried as part of their insignia by certain officers of the crown.

reverend Respectable.

tipped ... horn Usually 'horn-handled', but with the usual implication of the risk of cuckolding if the 'support' is a wife.

ta'en Captured.

brave Suitable.

Revision questions on Act V

1 Give an account of Benedick's delivery of his challenge to Claudio and its reception.

2 How is Don John's plot uncovered? Give an account of the parts played in this by (a) Dogberry and (b) Borachio.

3 In what ways do you find Beatrice and Benedick still the focus of our attention in Act V?

4 What dramatic or other effects are produced by Act V Scene 3?

5 Do you find the ending of the play satisfactory?

Shakespeare's art in *Much Ado About Nothing*
The characters

Beatrice (she who blesses)

. . . but then there was a star danced, and under that was I born.

Beatrice is one of the most independent and modern of Shakespeare's heroines. She begins the 'merry war' with Benedick, and indeed her first words in the play mock him. She speaks in sequences of imagery – killed, eaten, musty victual, trencher-man, stomach – which indicate the quickness and fertility of her imagination. She is never at a loss for words; but words cover the pathos of loneliness which is several times hinted at in the play. Early on, however, we do not suspect this, for she takes up any innocent reply and turns it into innuendo, often of a sexual nature. One of her salient features is the ability to laugh at herself. Her wit is reinforced by her imagination, and often takes the form of a pun or play on words. Her first overt exchange with Benedick is frosty, at times blunt to the point of physical insult 'Scratching could not make it worse', and 'twere such a face as yours were' but generally her wit, like that of her opponent in this verbal fencing, is intellectual, brilliant, sparkling with ideas and associations, frequently bawdy. This in a sense shows the extent of her modernity. She will let no man put her down in the verbal or physical sense. Her independence is shown in her determination to choose for herself but, by an irony of plot manipulation, she has choice thrust upon her. Yet we suspect, such is the subtlety of the verbal texture of *Much Ado About Nothing*, that she is attracted to Benedick and that he is the only man who is her equal, his verbal sparks igniting hers and hers igniting his, both symbolic of consummation rather than war.

Beatrice is human because she is able to stoop – she runs close to the ground 'like a lapwing' – to overhear conversation which she knows concerns herself. Here she parallels Benedick; despite their intellectual and supposedly satiric verve, they each have the common touch and, more than this, the common humanity which deserts Claudio. We should note and respect, indeed feel warmly about, Beatrice's loyalty to Hero and her concern for her. When Hero is slandered by Claudio, she is the first to say, without fear of consequence and without any doubting (compare Leonato's reaction) 'O, on my soul, my cousin is belied!' This spontaneous reaction is endearing, for Beatrice here shows that she is intuitively right. She does not pause to think; her assurance speaks for itself. Crisis finds the real Beatrice and, although she has further exchanges with Benedick, she never looks back. Her 'Kill Claudio' is one of the most dramatic – and most frightening – moments in the play. She has in fact the heart of a man, and her language of passionate denunciation of Claudio reflects this – 'O God, that I were a man! I would eat his heart in the market-place' – while she also completely overcomes Benedick by the demand that he challenge Claudio. The mask – I choose the word deliberately – has fallen; the woman is revealed when the cosmetic gloss of her social language has faded.

The measure of successful characterization in drama, as in the novel, is to be found in our wish to be involved with that character and to have his/her presence before us. Much of the play goes slowly when Beatrice and Benedick are absent. At the beginning of Act II Beatrice ranges wittily over the question of a husband for herself, and even more wittily over the prospect of entering heaven, where St Peter 'shows me where the bachelors sit, and there live we as merry as the day is long'. It is a tantalizing picture, typical of Beatrice's imaginative verve. As always, she is guilty of verbal promiscuity but nothing more. She realizes the difference between herself and Hero in terms of a woman's duty, though she urges Hero to make an independent choice. Her own wit is expended on 'wooing, wedding, and repenting', but this gives place to a war of words when she and Benedick are masked. She generally gets the better of this baiting, speaking of Benedick to his (masked) face as 'the Prince's jester, a very dull fool'. This is a social as well as a verbal slap. But there is another revealing moment later in this scene which looks back to a past when, Beatrice appears to say, Benedick trifled with her affections after she had given him twice the love he gave her – 'I gave him use for it, a double heart for his single one.' This might well account for the tinctured bitterness which sometimes shows through in her verbal berating of Benedick. Yet perhaps we should look at it cautiously, and ask whether Beatrice would be likely to respond so readily to the news that Benedick loves her if she has already been hurt by him.

Her capacity for improvisation even to the point of flirtation with Don Pedro is winningly undertaken after Don Pedro has won Hero for Claudio. Beatrice is happy on her cousin's account, but turns the occasion to her own professed deprivation by saying 'I may sit in a corner and cry "Heigh-ho" for a husband!' This leads to Don Pedro's 'Will you have me, lady', which prompts Beatrice both to wit and to self-confession:

No, my lord, unless I might have another for working days: your Grace is too costly to wear everyday. But I beseech your Grace pardon me, I was born to speak all mirth and no matter.

There is a pathetic hint here of a wish, unvoiced but present, to perhaps be loved as Hero is. Her exit shortly afterwards gives rise to the feeling that she may have been somewhat overcome by her emotion. Be that as it may, the plot is soon engineered through the imagination of Don Pedro to bring her and Benedick together. We feel that each of them hears what they really want to hear. Beatrice's response – she is nothing if not impetuous – is immediate. She will not only repay Benedick's love, she will tame 'my wild heart to thy loving hand'. Her mockery of marriage is overturned on the instant and without proof and once again we have to suspend our disbelief. Like Benedick, Beatrice goes into a melancholy and even here she is outjoked by Margaret and Hero.

The denunciation of Hero has already been considered in the context of Beatrice, but we should note her honesty – and in view of her strength of feeling she could easily have lied – in saying that for the first time in a year she had not spent the night with Hero. In the aftermath of that denunciation Beatrice comes dangerously near to confessing her love for Benedick; she does however make a 'temporary' confession in order to persuade Benedick to challenge Claudio. There is a moment in Act V Scene 4 when we sense that Beatrice and Benedick may not come together but, as Benedick says, 'our own hands against our hearts', ironically their written as distinct from their spoken words, bring them together.

Beatrice has good sense and a kind and loyal nature; she is also considerate, as she shows after she has talked to the Messenger in Act I Scene 1. Here, seeing that he does not understand her innuendoes with regard to Benedick, she tries to put him at his ease. She is lively, spirited, alert, but, as we have seen, she has a serious side. Of course she is intelligent too, sympathetic, warm though not, perhaps, as lovable as Viola in *Twelfth Night* or Rosalind in *As You Like It*. But both these latter are vulnerable, particularly because they are disguised as men; Beatrice is never disguised, though her mask of words sometimes conceals the warmth of her affections and her need to be loved.

Benedick (he who is blessed)

Here you may see Benedick, the married man

Benedick has many of the qualities of Beatrice. He is witty but is also kind and considerate, he is not lacking in courage – witness his challenge to Claudio – and he has the human frailty to want to listen to a conversation about himself. Determined to remain a bachelor or rather at least superficially subscribing to a cynical view of marriage, he is easily baited and then caught. Like Beatrice's wit, his is intellectual, stringent, sometimes boastful and often contains sexual allusions. Until he learns of Beatrice's 'love' for him he enjoys the war of words, but after that he succumbs to a period of melancholy – almost the statutory mood for romantic lovers – before surfacing into activity with his challenge to Claudio. He is vulnerable, impressionable, reading into Beatrice's coming to summon him into dinner signs of the love he has just overheard that she feels for him. 'I do spy some sparks of love in her' he observes, and he also shaves off his beard, probably because he has heard that Beatrice 'could not endure a husband with a beard on his face'.

Benedick's interchanges with Beatrice reflect his wit, but he generally comes off worse, Beatrice being adept at having the last word. With Claudio he is satirical about the merits of Hero, playing on words like 'low', 'brown' and 'little' with antithetical verve. He refers to his own conquests, speaking of himself as 'a professed tyrant to their sex', but whether these are real or imagined we do not know. Suffice to say that as early as the first scene he unwittingly (I use the word deliberately) indicates the ultimate track of his inclinations, referring to Beatrice as exceeding Hero 'in beauty as the first of May doth the last of December'. Nonetheless his determination to remain a bachelor is forcibly expressed and so reiterated that one suspects it provokes Don Pedro and Claudio to fashion the plot to get Benedick married to Beatrice. In the masked dance of Act II Scene 1 he is well and truly put down by Beatrice, but his reaction (he tries to laugh it off afterwards and even considers that Beatrice didn't know who she was talking to) is to tell Claudio that 'the Prince hath got your Hero'. Now either Benedick believes this or, and this seems a little more likely, he is teasing Claudio. This illustrates Benedick's capacity for making the most of any situation verbally, but he soon recurs to Beatrice's treatment of himself. He says 'I would not marry her, though she were endowed with all that Adam had left him before he transgressed.' For all his verbal screens, Benedick does not know himself.

Benedick's superb soliloquy at the beginning of Act II Scene 3 again finds him pondering on love, here complacently comparing himself to the smitten Claudio, little knowing that he is just about to hear that Beatrice loves him. He expatiates upon the graces he would expect to find in a woman – she must be fair, wise and virtuous – but he adds that she must be mild, 'of good discourse, an excellent musician'. All this is forgotten when he learns of Beatrice's love. Here he reveals his own conceit and a certain lack of insight, for he accepts that he is not being gulled since Leonato, 'the white-bearded fellow' is conveying Beatrice's feelings largely through the reportage of Hero. He quickly decides that Beatrice's love must be 'requited', and admits that she is wise, fair and virtuous, thus conveniently finding in her the qualities he requires in a woman. It is a remarkable *volte face*, but of a piece with the nature of this comedy, which is based on deception and, in part, on self-deception.

Benedick, soldier and courtier, is transformed by this new knowledge. 'Gallants, I am not as I have been', he says, and ascribes his sadness to the toothache. The church scene finds Benedick responding to Beatrice's assertion of Hero's innocence and also examining the situation compassionately (with regard to Hero) and practically (by asking Beatrice if she had spent the previous night with Hero). In fact Benedick acts sensibly and nobly, telling Leonato:

Yet, by mine honour, I will deal in this
As secretly and justly as your soul
Should with your body. (Act IV, Scene 1)

From this he switches to consoling Beatrice, even admitting – and the admission is not without pathos – 'I do love nothing in the world so well as you – is not that strange?' Pressed by Beatrice he agrees to challenge Claudio; this is a measure of his love for Beatrice and his belief in Hero's innocence. He passes Beatrice's test to prove his love and is prepared to risk his life. Pale when he delivers the challenge to Claudio – after all, he could hardly expect to enjoy fighting his best friend – Benedick remains firm and noble. His words to Claudio embody real feeling as distinct from imposed wit; they are brief, telling, just, despite the fact that the lie of Hero's 'death' is embedded in his accusation of Claudio. He is angered by Claudio's and Don Pedro's baiting of him re Beatrice, for he calls Claudio 'Boy' and also, ironically, 'Lord Lackbeard', but he bids Don Pedro a dignified farewell. Benedick, we remember, had been the first to trace the church denunciation scene to the machinations of Don John. Benedick's treatment of Margaret, who almost replaces Beatrice as a verbal fencer in Act V Scene 2, has a certain self-consciousness about it; he does what is expected of him by responding to her sexual innuendoes with his own, but even here we feel that what he says of his words, that they are a 'most manly wit' is true. There is another dimension to Benedick the romantic lover, for unlike the general run of romantic lovers Benedick was 'not born under a rhyming planet', and feels the failure keenly. His final exchanges with Beatrice reflect the casting away of the masks; what they have written reveals their hearts more surely than anything they have overheard. Benedick, the now to be married man, embraces marriage joyously, his insistence on the dancing reflecting happiness and natural celebration now that he has found his natural partner.

Claudio

> O, what men dare do! What men may do!
> What men daily do, not knowing what they do!

Claudio is obsessed with his own honour, and there are times in the play when he seems to be more a character of tragedy than of comedy. We learn almost immediately the play opens that he has conducted himself bravely in battle, 'doing, in the figure of a lamb, the feats of a lion'. His entrance passes almost unnoticed, since Beatrice and Benedick are soon into their verbal war. Left alone with Benedick, Claudio confesses his feelings for Hero and, after Benedick's exit, launches into poetry in order to convey these feelings to Don Pedro:

> But now I am return'd, and that war-thoughts
> Have left their places vacant, in their rooms
> Come thronging soft and delicate desires,
> All prompting me how fair young Hero is,
> Saying I lik'd her ere I went to wars. (Act I Scene 1)

Claudio is always highly self-conscious. We feel that this is a sentimental love, that he is indulging himself; strangely, he makes no response when Don Pedro says that he will woo Hero for Claudio, thought it is obviously Claudio's wish that Hero's feelings towards himself should be revealed before he ventures to reveal his own. There is something odd about the fact that he makes no direct approach to Hero, and does not speak to her before he sees her in the church. It is a kind of vicarious courtship, but possessive nonetheless. When Benedick tells him 'the Prince hath got your

Hero' he accepts it as truth, just as a few minutes previously he had listened to – and accepted – Don John's cunning insinuation that Don Pedro is in love with Hero. This reveals the shallowness of Claudio's nature, a shallowness which is to be displayed again, and much more seriously, when he trusts his eyes over Hero's deception but hasn't the depth or the faith to trust her. When he hears Don Pedro say that he has won Hero for him (Claudio) he is baited by Beatrice to speak on cue, but says, and this certainly demonstrates his self-consciousness, 'Silence is the perfectest herald of joy.' He enters into the spirit of the gulling of Benedick, and we are made aware that Claudio does have a sense of humour. When the quieter Benedick presents himself, Claudio enjoys baiting him, gaining perhaps some small revenge for Benedick's mockery of him over Hero.

Claudio's shallowness, his gullibility – at variance with what we should expect of a valiant courtier – leads to the near tragedy of *Much Ado About Nothing*. Taking Don John's word that Hero is unfaithful, Claudio reacts vehemently to this threat to his honour, and immediately distances himself from audience and reader by undertaking the public revenge of denouncing Hero in church. Apparently he hasn't the wit to question Don John's statement, despite the latter's reputation; lacking in common-sense, he also appears to be lacking in spirit and certainly in life experience. In his self-conceit Claudio thinks more of the potential wrong done to himself than to the *honour* of Hero. Everything is seen from his own point of view and how it will affect him; on the slenderest of suggestions he is motivated to revenge and cruelty. Beatrice sees through him; to her he is 'civil as an orange, and something of that jealous complexion' and also 'Count Comfect; a sweet gallant'.

Claudio is discredited as a character by the church scene, for even if his accusation were true it would be a greater disgrace to him than to Hero. What is inexcusable is the nature of his language; Hero is now 'a rotten orange' while 'She knows the heat of a luxurious bed/Her blush is guiltiness, not modesty'; she is 'an approved wanton', 'a common stale'. Claudio carries his plan through without any compunction and it should be noted that his decision to denounce Hero publicly is taken *before* she is proven guilty.

After the denunciation Claudio renounces all thoughts of love – this is typical of his impetuosity – but the next morning, after learning from Leonato and Benedick that Hero is dead, he shows little concern. He rejects the somewhat ludicrous challenges of

Antonio and Leonato, says that he and Don Pedro 'are high-proof melancholy' and urges Benedick to 'use thy wit'. All this underlines the shallowness I have referred to earlier. He has courage enough to accept that Benedick is in deadly earnest in his challenge, but continues to jest even about this until the Watch produce Borachio, who confesses what he has done. Claudio reacts as usual in extremes, saying of Borachio's confession 'I have drunk poison whiles he utter'd it' and yet happy that Hero's image 'doth appear/In the rare semblance that I lov'd it first'. Such is Claudio's facile nature that we feel he will enjoy the melancholy of repentance! He quickly agrees however to marry Antonio's daughter (never having seen her). Having lamented Hero's death at Leonato's tomb with appropriate dirge and ritual (which he says he will undertake every year) Claudio looks forward to his coming wedding, accepts the fact that Hero is Hero, and expends some of his wit on Benedick becoming a married man.

Claudio himself gets more than he deserves. His presentation leaves a nasty taste; he has an eye to the main chance, establishing that Leonato has no son and that therefore Hero stands to inherit a fortune one day. He thinks only of himself, his reactions being superficial and unpleasant. We cannot at any stage in the play after the first scene feel that he is good enough for Hero.

Hero

she is the sweetest lady that I ever looked on

Hero is the nominal heroine of *Much Ado*. In terms of verbal power she is subordinate to Beatrice, indeed in the first scene of the play she has only one line, and this draws attention to the fact that Beatrice's jokes are at the expense of Benedick. We learn more of Hero from the impression she makes on Claudio in Act I. In Act II she is gentle, patient, self-possessed, with perhaps a slightly ironic humour as she talks to Don Pedro. She is an obedient daughter, obeying her father's instructions as to how she shall treat her lover. Much pathos attends Hero, and some near tragedy. She gets caught up in the central joke of the play in the attempt to get Beatrice and Benedick to marry; here her response is prim, for she tells Don Pedro that 'I will do any modest office, my lord, to help my cousin to a good husband.'

In fact Hero does more than that. Generally she follows where others lead, and shows little initiative. But in the duping of Beatrice Hero plays the leading role and plays it with verve and vivacity too. She despatches Margaret to acquaint Beatrice with the fact that she is the central subject of the conversation between Ursula and Hero; that faked conversation shows Hero's intelligence and her insight into Beatrice:

> her wit
> Values itself so highly that to her
> All matter else seems weak. (Act III, Scene 1)

Hero pulls no verbal punches; the listening Beatrice gets a portrait of herself that is far from flattering. Hero even goes so far as to tell Ursula that she will go to Benedick and urge him to fight against his passion for Beatrice and, cunningly, says just how highly she rates Benedick herself. Here she is seconded by Ursula, and departs with the line 'Some Cupid kills with arrows, some with traps.'

We do not see this spirited and playful Hero again. In Act III Scene 4 as she prepares for her wedding she has a sense of foreboding; she hardly responds to Margaret's teasing, just notices that Beatrice too is out of sorts, and reverts to her usual role of saying very little. When Claudio condemns her she behaves at first with dignity, and always with modesty and propriety; she assumes that Claudio must be unwell to make such wild accusations. Her denial is simple and moving and of course we know that it is true, as true as the swoon which follows. We feel the pathos, a terrible pathos, that Hero should be doubted not only by her lover but by her father. Yet she agrees without question to the Friar's plan, and accepts her lover back without questioning his disloyalty. In the final scene a little touch of Hero's sportive spirit is revealed, for she has stolen one of Beatrice's letters from her pocket, and reveals its contents, which demonstrate Beatrice's love for Benedick.

In most things, though, she is too good to be true. Hero never utters an unkind word, not even to Claudio; she obviously looks up to him just as she looks up to her father, having nothing of Beatrice's independence in what she, Hero, obviously regards as a man's world. Her forgiveness of Claudio does involve a generosity of spirit but, love or no love, she would have married him out of duty anyway. She appears to have no resentment of Beatrice or of anyone else, but she is not completely insipid. There is a kind of life when she is gulling Beatrice with Ursula, a kind of modesty, nobility, acceptance in her suffering, but little positive animation when she is in the company of her elders.

Don Pedro

Be happy, lady, for you are like an honourable father

The Prince of Aragon has individuality and a major function in the plot of the play. He is immediately kind to Leonato, and has honoured Claudio as a reward for his services. He intends to stay a month with Leonato, and this enables him to court Hero on Claudio's account, and to instigate the plot to bring Beatrice and Benedick together. He wields some authority, finding out from Benedick about Claudio's feelings for Hero. He obviously approves his choice, and takes some innocent delight in the 'courtship' himself. Before that he crosses verbal swords with Benedick, prophesying that Benedick will one day be sick with love. His plan over Hero is quite straightforward; he will pretend to be Claudio (all the guests will be masked) and reveal Claudio's love to Hero. Although he is suspected by Don John and by Claudio at one stage of wooing for himself, Don Pedro is in fact honest, honourable, nobly-intentioned. He takes real pleasure in having obtained Hero for Claudio and, that plan having been successful, promises Beatrice that he will get her a husband. He quickly enlists the support of Claudio, Leonato and Hero in the gulling of Beatrice and Benedick. He reveals that he is a consummate actor, repeating his lines, which lure Benedick into believing that Beatrice loves him, with relish. He is intent on putting down Benedick and elevating Beatrice, even indicating that he would have liked to have Beatrice in love with himself. He then organizes through Leonato 'the same net spread for her'. He joins in the mockery of the melancholy Benedick, but surprisingly accepts the word of his bastard brother Don John that Hero has been unfaithful. He even allows himself to say that he will join with Claudio in the public disgrace of Hero if her disloyalty is proved. Leonato's appeal to the 'Sweet Prince' finds the latter only too ready to say that Hero is 'a common stale'. Later accosted by an enraged Leonato and Antonio, Don Pedro behaves with much more dignity than Claudio, and with much more compassion, even telling Leonato 'My heart is sorry for your daughter's death', but with the arrival of Benedick he resorts to levity in his description of the two old men who have just tried to duel with them. He even baits Benedick by supposedly quoting Beatrice, but is later sharp enough to note that Benedick has revealed that Don John has fled. When Conrade and Borachio are produced bound before him, he has a delightful time mocking Dogberry's mode of address by parodying it. Don Pedro's humiliation is near at hand when Borachio confesses but, like

Claudio, he is willing to undertake penance. Don Pedro has much more about him than Claudio, generously acting on the latter's behalf and having rather more wit and ingenuity than that 'exquisite' man. But he exists with Claudio on that unpleasantly superficial level of the play; he, the duper, is duped by Borachio and by his own brother. His noble qualities do come to the fore though, and at least he has the humility to admit his error.

Leonato

This good old man

Leonato is a good host, welcoming the victors to his house and offering them suitable entertainment. He even includes Don John, and we must also remember that he has given his niece Beatrice a home. We feel that he is flattered by Don Pedro's presence, and he is quick not only to advise Hero but to join in the gulling of Benedick. Leonato's role here convinces Benedick of the truth of what he hears, since he feels that Leonato would not take part in any duplicity. He enjoys taking part in verbal duels with Benedick, giving as good as he gets and sometimes better. He seems to be kindly and tolerant, even having the courtesy to explain to the Messenger in the first scene the nature of the 'merry war' between Beatrice and Benedick. Leonato's greeting of Don Pedro is both courteous and elaborate, but he is cautious when his brother Antonio tells him that a servant of his has overheard that Don Pedro is in love with Hero. Not only is he cautious, he is also careful to see that Hero gets this piece of news. He indulges in witticisms with Beatrice, of whom he is obviously fond, and then, hoping perhaps that Don Pedro will court Hero for himself, counsels Hero to accept him if he does. He cheerfully accepts Claudio and arranges the marriage, and shrewdly comments on Beatrice and Benedick – 'if they were but a week married, they would talk themselves mad.'

His part in the gulling of Benedick is an important one. He is almost like a child in his enthusiasm 'I am for you, though it cost me ten nights' watchings' and contributes to Hero's supposed reportage of Beatrice's deep love for Benedick. He calls Dogberry 'honest neighbour', delegating his authority to him on what is his daughter's wedding-day. The day, however, is ruined, and Leonato's reactions are both pitiable and censurable. His love for Hero is unquestionable 'Bring me a father that so loved his child' but the evidence against Hero is damning, and in any case he believes Don Pedro and Claudio to be honourable men. Because of this he joins in the accusations against his own daughter; here he is a victim of deception but also less than a loyal and loving father when he most needs to be. He rallies at Benedick's belief that this is a plot of Don John's, and his humiliation and mortification turn to angry thoughts of revenge. He agrees to the Friar's plan, holding fast to the 'smallest twine' perhaps more in despair than hope. Soon his great trust in Hero reasserts itself and, with a courage that belies his years, he challenges Claudio. He also has to deal with his brother's aggressiveness towards Claudio and Don Pedro and is concerned that Antonio should not get hurt. He generously forgives Claudio after Don John's plot has been revealed but is suspicious of Margaret's role in that plot. His generosity of spirit also embraces Don Pedro and, before Hero is unmasked and revealed as herself, he replies to the Friar's 'Did I not tell you she was innocent?':

So are the Prince and Claudio, who accus'd her
Upon the error that you heard debated.

Leonato is indeed a good old man, and even lets Benedick have his own way in his (Leonato's) house by allowing him the dance he so wants.

Don John

I had rather be a canker in a hedge than a rose in his grace.

Don John is the stage villain of *Much Ado About Nothing*. His motivations are jealousy of his half-brother Don Pedro (and of Claudio's advance in that brother's affections too) and revenge. His first words are token words of thanks, striking the keynote of his character, for they are sulky, morose, grudging. He is an embittered man, and has recently rebelled openly, and been defeated. He determines to be revenged on Don Pedro for his encouragement of the young 'start-up' Claudio. The knowledge of Claudio's impending marriage affords him the opportunity of getting back at Don Pedro through his new favourite. He has little or no standing, and associates with followers who can be relied upon to obey his every whim. His bastardy makes him feel inferior anyway, and the only way he can assert his frustrated power is by employing people in the service of his evil. His inferiority is reflected in his claim of others that 'Their cheer is the greater that I am subdued.'

Using the means of deception that are conveniently at his command – the masks – he tells Claudio whom he deliberately names as Benedick that Don Pedro is 'enamoured on Hero'. Not content with this, he lends an eager ear to Borachio's plot to discredit Hero. He fully exploits the gullibility of Don Pedro and Claudio and, but for Borachio's free-talking, would have succeeded in his scheming. Naturally he flees to save his own skin.

Much Ado has a dark side to its comedy and Don John's character, taken with Claudio's denunciation of Hero, smacks of sickness. The fact that he has no status and feels that he ought to have accounts for his actions, but his moroseness appears to be a character trait. One understands his resentment of Claudio once one comes to know Claudio, but his deliberate lack of concern over Hero puts him beyond any sympathy we might feel. He is a sad soured man.

Antonio

An old man

Antonio appears in three scenes. In the first he reports, whether mistakenly or genuinely is not known, that his servant has overheard Don Pedro saying that he loves Hero. This is the first of the rumours which are false with regard to the courtship. Antonio has little personality of his own, and is largely a foil to Leonato. His attempt to engage Claudio in a duel is ridiculous, almost grotesque, and Leonato is obviously embarrassed by it. Antonio had previously advised patience, but here becomes so enraged himself that he has to be restrained.

Conrade and Borachio

Proof enough to misuse the Prince, to vex Claudio, to undo Hero, and kill Leonato.

These followers of Don John are functional to the plot of *Much Ado About Nothing* and Borachio in particular has a strong personality. Since so much of the play depends on what is overheard, Borachio is part of the structural coherence. He 'whipped me behind the arras' and heard that Don Pedro is to woo Hero for Claudio (accurate reportage here!) and from this incident he evolves the plot to discredit Hero with the (unwitting?) help of Margaret. Borachio is unscrupulous and inventive, suggesting to Don John that he should tell Claudio and Don Pedro that Hero loves him (Borachio). He even undertakes to so 'fashion the matter that Hero shall be absent'. He has the nerve and the courage to carry it through. He obviously takes great pride in being Don John's right-hand man but, free-speaking in drink (the name Borachio means 'drunkard', a deliberate irony on Shakespeare's part) gives himself away. Yet there is another side to him which, in this play of deception, makes us sympathetic towards this man whose conscience is pricked. He confesses his crime with the utmost clarity and frankness, and that confession implies regret. Even more commendable is the way that he springs to Margaret's defence when Leonato seeks to apportion equal blame to her for the betrayal of Hero:

> No, by my soul she was not!
> Nor knew not what she did when she spoke to me,
> But always hath been just and virtuous
> In anything that I do know by her.

It is noble, honourable behaviour – behaviour beyond the reach of his master and, ironically, beyond the reach of Claudio. Borachio stands by the woman who has helped him but clears her unequivocally! He shoulders the whole blame. He is not a servant but, initially twisted, a gentleman. Conrade too is a gentleman (he reminds Dogberry of this fact) but he is much less positive than Borachio. He is more the philosopher than the man of action, though he indulges in word-play with Borachio which underpins the main word-play elements of the plot. It is Borachio who does the planning and the talking, and Conrade is largely a foil to him.

Friar Francis

Have comfort, lady

Friar Francis is another functional character, representing goodness and commonsense; he cools things down after the denunciation scene, counselling Hero to look up and providing, in his spiritual and temporal soundness, an insight into the reasons for her swoon. Just as Borachio fashions a black comedy plan, so Friar Francis devises a plan which he hopes will uncover the truth and lead to repentance on behalf of the guilty parties. His exhortations in Act IV Scene 1 are both noble and practical, despite the fact that they involve deception. He misreads slightly the effect of the announcement of Hero's 'death' on Claudio and the Prince, since Leonato's anger provokes Claudio when Hero's 'death' is laid at his door.

Margaret and Ursula

Give us the swords, we have bucklers of our own.

Margaret is a most positive character, her wit, often bawdy, rivalling that of Beatrice. Both are gentlewomen, with Margaret showing a rare capacity for teasing in Act III Scene 4. First of all she takes a delight in Hero's clothes for the wedding, and then proceeds to lighten Hero's heart by saying that "Twill be the heavier soon by the weight of a man". She calls this kind of wit 'true speaking', and descants upon it with the arrival of a 'heavy' Beatrice. She sees into Beatrice's love for Benedick (we remember that she is part of the deception here anyway), and later enjoys a satirical bout with Benedick in which she employs her bawdy bent to the full. The one question-mark against Margaret is her entering into the deception by impersonating Hero at Borachio's instigation. This is done off-stage but it is fraught with consequences and, though Borachio bears eloquent testimony to her virtue, we cannot help but feel that for one so sharp she is curiously lacking insight at a critical juncture. The impression we get is that Margaret enjoys a joke but is irresponsible and uncritical of her own actions. Ursula is merely a foil to Hero in the deception of Beatrice, going along with all that is said and adding in provocative remarks which are calculated to move the listening Beatrice to love for Benedick.

Dogberry and Verges

But, masters, remember that I am an ass.

Dogberry and Verges are clowns, fools who accidently hit on the discovery which changes the course of events in the play. Neither is seen in any depth, but the actions of these two and the Watch provide farcical verbal and situation comedy which balances the sophisticated word-play and deceptions of the nobility. There is a definite and undisguised Englishness about them. Dogberry is the name of a wild shrub, and the implication is that he remains 'wild' in his abuse of language. He is a little man elevated – and elevating himself – to a temporary position of authority. We laugh at him as well as with him. His malapropisms lend a farcical tone to the scenes in which he appears. His briefing of the Watch in Act III Scene 2 strikes just such a note. He interrupts, bullies, misunderstands at will; yet curiously, and deliberately, he is linked by Shakespeare with the main verbal artists of the play. Benedick and Beatrice take great pride in their wit and are insulted if its quality is questioned; Dogberry takes great pride in his wisdom, is self-opinionated and certainly thinks he is clever, so that he is a mirror of the fully articulate characters by virtue of his own deadly ability to articulate inaccurately. Moreover, just as they are often verbose, so is he; whereas their verbosity is self-indulgent, his is too but it is also a measure of his incompetence. Full of self-importance ('you shall comprehend all vagrom men') and bluster, he rests on cowardice ('take no note of him, but let him go'). He has an inherent wit that is not dependent on the mismanagement of words, though whether he is aware of it is unlikely:

The most peaceable way for you, if you do take a thief, is to let him show himself what he is, and steal out of your company. (Act III, Scene 3)

He is full of pretence as well as pretentiousness, for when the Sexton points out to him that he does not know the law well enough to conduct an examination of prisoners correctly, he asserts that he knew all the time 'Yea, marry, that's the eftest way'. Because he talks so much little is discovered except by chance. Verges tries to drive the point home to Leonato, whereas Dogberry, in his own condescension to Verges 'A good old man, sir, he will be talking' virtually ensures that he will have to conduct the 'excommunication' of the prisoners himself since Leonato is in a hurry to get to the wedding. Dogberry's capacity for total irrelevance is seen in his questioning of Borachio and Conrade, and he reaches the heights of absurdity in his famous 'Dost thou not suspect my place? Dost thou not suspect my years? O that he were here to write me down as ass!' (Act IV Scene 2). He has an exchange with Don Pedro which shows that he cannot count, and exits from the play bowing and scraping.

Neighbour Verges is the foil to Dogberry, almost in the tradition of the knockabout comedian pair. He asks the questions which allow Dogberry to pontificate, or he echoes Dogberry's remarks. He has little idea of what to do, though he is able to tell the Watch how to behave if they hear a child crying in the night – 'You must call to the nurse and bid her still it.' Dogberry feeds on Verges' admiration, but soon puts him down if he gets too independent and seems about to usurp his superior authority. The Watch were stock subjects of satire in the Elizabethan period but, although they provoke laughter, they are drawn with affection. The satire is good-humoured, without ill-feeling or bitterness; though muddle ensues, even Leonato is moved to thank Dogberry and Verges for their 'care and honest pains'.

Theme, atmosphere and setting

Theme

The major theme of *Much Ado About Nothing* is that of deception. False report, generally of hearsay or overhearing, is the key to this. There is of course also the serious misapprehension arising from false 'seeing' which, though it takes place off-stage, changes, albeit temporarily, a ceremony of marriage into a virulent scene of condemnation. Antonio falsely reports to Leonato that a man of his has overheard Don Pedro tell Claudio that he is in love with Hero. This is the first of the confusions, which can either be interpreted as innocent or, in view of Antonio's bumbling nature, misinformed. This occurs in Act I Scene 2, and in the following scene, Borachio gives Don John the information – and therefore the fuel to ignite a plot – that Don Pedro is to woo Hero for himself and then hand her over to Don John. This is merely a slight distortion, since Don Pedro is to woo her in Claudio's name and then get her father's consent. Borachio in fact tells Don John that Claudio is intent on marriage with Hero, so that this variant prepares us for the deceptions of Claudio by Don John and, strangely, by Benedick, both of whom tell Claudio that Don Pedro woos for himself. They are wrong, the first maliciously so, but the effect is to heighten the dramatic tension, with Claudio's own doubts and our own response to them and the situation.

It can be argued that a large part of Act II Scene 1 consists of deception, since once the dancers are masked there is the dual deception of pretending to know who you are talking to and the more serious corollary of knowing who you are talking to but deliberately adopting a pose. For example, while Don Pedro 'courts' Hero, Beatrice tells Benedick a few home truths about himself while affecting not to know who he is. Thus she is able to continue their 'merry war' of words on her own terms. Don John affects to be talking to Benedick – he knows he is talking to Claudio – in order to say that he knows Don Pedro is courting Hero for himself; Borachio reinforces this with his 'So did I too, and he swore he would marry her tonight.' Benedick follows with his own 'for the Prince hath got your Hero' (is it part of his wit to tease Claudio?) and then congratulates himself 'that my Lady Beatrice should know me and not know me'. Later he adds to this by telling Don Pedro 'She told me, not thinking I had been myself, that I was the Prince's jester.' The effects of duplicity so far subserve the dramatic structure of the play; Claudio is gullible, Benedick is gullible with regard to Beatrice, and both are to have that gullibility further exposed by two plots of deception, the one evil, the other cunningly designed to effect a marriage and not break one.

The next important deception gets under way by the end of the same scene when Don Pedro observes of Beatrice 'She were an excellent wife for Benedick.' Following this the dual gulling occurs, but not before Don John, stimulated by Borachio, has determined to undertake the plot suggested by his cunning follower to discredit Hero. This is in Act II Scene 2, and hot upon it comes the deception of Benedick. Balthasar sings an appropriate song to put Benedick in the mood to believe that he is loved, and his respect for Leonato's age provides Benedick with the assurance he needs to believe what he is hearing. The motivation for this deception – and remember that Leonato is fond of his niece – would appear to be a mixture of goodness and sheer pleasure at seeing two people (Benedick and Beatrice) ultimately eat their own words. The deception of course involves the constant hyperbole that Beatrice loves Benedick, and an exact parallel is followed by Hero and Ursula in their elaborate exchanges which convince the listening Beatrice that Benedick is passionately in love with her. But lest we forget the evil of Don John, there immediately follows the scene (Act III Scene 2) in which Don John tells Don Pedro and Claudio – note the strength of this, since Don Pedro can vouch for what Claudio is to 'see' – that Hero is disloyal and that they shall see her disloyalty demonstrated.

The introduction of the Watch brings a new dimension to the quality of deception. Here it is the delusion of local grandeur which is being presented, self-deception in the use of words and competence, with the irony that Conrade and Borachio are themselves to be discovered – deceived in their sense of security – by amateurs who have overheard the professional execution of the deception plot. Again we are aware of the depths at which Shakespeare is working. That the Watch are not deceived is through no fault of their own – indeed, one wonders whether Dogberry himself would have apprehended Conrade and Borachio or have been capable of understanding what was being said. For Dogberry, as we know, is deceived by words. When the sexton asks 'Which be the malefactors?' Dogberry answers with all the assurance in the world 'Marry, that am I and my partner.' The deception throughout the Dogberry scenes is a verbal one and underlines the main deceptions in the play.

After seeing the evidence of his own eyes – and of course he is deceived – Claudio denounces Hero. Swift upon this follows another deception, for the Friar's plot to announce the death of Hero sets in train the next sequence of deception. Here the motive is unquestionably good. Claudio and Don Pedro are deceived, though their first reception to the news of Hero's 'death' could hardly be described as sympathetic. The discovery that they have been deceived comes with Borachio's confession. And even after this the deception continues. Leonato is intent, albeit rather unrealistically, on the marriage finally coming about, and makes the condition of Claudio's repentance marriage with his 'niece'. That niece is of course the 'living' Hero, and Claudio is further deceived into hanging up a scroll for the 'dead' Hero ('Done to death by slanderous tongues/Was the Hero that here lies.') All is revealed, but the corollary of deception continues in the Beatrice and Benedick plot in the latter's 'Here's our own hands against our hearts' with the deception of the stealing of their writings to each other confessing love.

It will be seen from all this how much the play depends on deception, told or designed to be overheard or seen, both in the serious side of the plot involving Claudio and Hero and in the comic plots, all interwoven, involving Beatrice and Benedick and Dogberry and the Watch. Don John's role is that of arch-deceiver, but he is ironically himself deceived by the unexpected integrity of one of his followers, Borachio.

Atmosphere

Although the fundamental atmosphere is that of humorous and witty interchange (buttressed upon the deception that we have noticed as the main ingredient of the play) there is an underlying tragic motif in *Much Ado About Nothing* which is typical of Shakespeare in his comedies - we think of Shylock and his situation in *The Merchant of Venice,* or of the feud between Duke Senior and Duke Frederick in *As You Like It,* or the treatment of Malvolio in *Twelfth Night.* The word tragic here is used in its potential rather than real sense – we are aware of what might have been rather than what actually is in the resolution of the play's action. Thus on the morning of Hero's wedding there is an atmosphere of impending tragedy. She is herself heavy of heart and Margaret's badinage cannot lighten her foreboding. That foreboding is fully realized by the unbridled insensitivity of Claudio's language to her and to Leonato, made the more terrible and poignant by the fact that it is uttered in church. Nothing is sacred to Claudio except his honour.

As in Shakespeare's much later play, *Cymbeline,* a woman is unjustly slandered and her lover rejects her. There all is cleared up largely by divine intervention; here, in *Much Ado About Nothing*, it is cleared up by the characters themselves, largely through the agency of the representative of God, the Friar. But the rejection and its aftermath, the supposed death and its aftermath, trace a path from near-tragedy to reconciliation, a path which Shakespeare was later to follow with nearly the same dramatic intensity in *The Winter's Tale*. Hero's anxiety before the church scene evokes a dramatic response from reader and audience, since they know of Don John's plot and of Claudio's vow to publicly condemn Hero. But the sense of tragedy is superbly balanced by comic relief. For example, Don John's plot to discredit Hero is followed by two scenes involving the Watch, who have discovered Borachio and Conrade. This is in Act III, and the church scene is in fact in Act IV Scene 1. The Watch actually tell Leonato what they have done but, because of his haste to get to the wedding, he tells Dogberry to undertake the examination of the prisoners himself. The atmosphere now is one of indescribable tension, since had Leonato stayed and listened, the denunciation scene would never have occurred. This shows Shakespeare's mastery of dramatic irony, one of the major ingredients in sustaining and projecting atmosphere. Together in this play, co-existing in a kind of counterpoint to each other, we have tragic power, gaiety and revelry, wit, a variety of comedy and, ultimately, happy romance. These constitute the atmospheres, ever blending and changing, of *Much Ado About Nothing*. Sunshine and clouds are never far away from each other, and it is part of the continuing atmosphere that it is sometimes hard to distinguish where one ends and the other begins.

Setting

Apart from the English histories, where location is based on fact and is therefore specifically English, the great majority of Shakespeare's plays are set in places abroad – Venice, Verona, an island, Rome, Illyria, Sicilia and Bohemia, to name but a few. This device in itself tends to give them a romantic colouring. The local colour, however, is generally that of Elizabethan England, the life and spirit of the play providing the various levels of the audience with a reflection or projection of their own lives and experiences, the appeal being human rather than instructive (though it may well have been). In the Elizabethan period most of the audience who saw the plays would be untravelled and often uneducated, and anachronisms or improbabilities would not be subject for comment or disparity in an age more familiar with stories than with their settings. The nominal setting for *Much Ado About Nothing* is Messina, but we are never far removed from Elizabethan England, the England of Shakespeare and his audience.

Shakespeare's setting, though primarily in the upper orders at Leonato's house or in church, embraces something of a social spectrum through the Watch, the policemen of the day whose turns of duty (after their ordinary jobs were over) were at night or in case of emergency. Their setting is the street (Act III, Scene 3), Leonato's house (Act III, Scene 5) where they arrive with the news of the apprehension of some 'arrant knaves', and the prison (Act IV, Scene 2) where the Sexton effectively sorts out their verbal bungling, arranges for the prisoners to be brought before Leonato, and gives the news that Don John has 'stolen away'. The authenticity of this Elizabethan setting and of Elizabethan practice is further enhanced by the reference to the 'gowns' they wear, which represent their office on official occasions.

The scenes at Leonato's house include the masked dance after supper, the kind of social occasion which was very popular at the time of the writing of *Much Ado About Nothing*. It was to become even more popular later in Shakespeare's life under the patronage of James I. Musicians were called 'attendants' (Act I, Scene 2), ballads were printed on broadsheets and circulated, and ballad-makers (mentioned with scorn by Benedick) ranked lower than musicians. There are three dances mentioned in conversation, one a 'Scotch jig' (surely incongruous in the Italy of Messina!), a 'cinque-pace' and a 'measure', all of them well-known Elizabethan dances which would be readily appreciated by the watching gentry and groundlings alike. Leonato's superior position of Governor would doubtless have an Elizabethan equivalent, something like that of a Lord of the Manor to whom the Watch are reporting.

The church scene also subserves to illustrate custom, since the words 'If either of you know any inward impediment . . .' are an echo of the words of the marriage service. Moreover, the garden scenes in the play have very much of an English flavour. The 'pleached bower' has an Italianate ring, but it is a bower of English 'honeysuckle'.

Structure and style

The structure of *Much Ado About Nothing* is straightforward in outline, rather more subtle and complex in its working out and interconnection. Basically there are main plots and sub-plots which interweave at particular points of crisis and resolution. The main plots comprise the Claudio-Hero story and the Benedick-Beatrice one. Here the characters are of noble birth, and the structural parallelism is balanced and contrasted at the same time. Claudio wishes to marry Hero who wishes to marry him; the marriage is at first prevented by a plot fronted by a character of part noble birth – Don John – and carried through by a character who is nominally much more than a servant but is in fact a time-serving follower, Borachio. Benedick and Beatrice are always overtly stating that they do not wish to marry (though Beatrice expresses a wish for a husband at one stage), and they are brought together by the machinations of characters of noble birth to marry in the end. The contrasts here will be apparent, and it must be emphasized that contrast is at the heart of Shakespearian drama.

The Borachio-Margaret sub-plot is initiated on stage and enacted off stage. The other sub-plot concerns Dogberry-Verges and it will be seen at once that both these reflect the main action. The crisis of the play – Act IV Scene 1 – is entirely dependent on the Borachio sub-plot. The discovery of that sub-plot is entirely due to the other sub-plot. Both are crucial to the first main plot, that of Claudio and Hero, and arguably affect the second main plot, since Beatrice's loyalty to Hero causes Benedick to challenge Claudio. Throughout the comic and the serious are brought into interaction with each other, just as they are in life, with Shakespeare heightening light and serious scenes by juxtaposition. Consider the clever patterning of scenes in the Claudio-Hero plot as against the Beatrice-Benedick plot, with the supreme irony that those who are trying (and succeeding) to deceive Beatrice and Benedick are in their turn deceived. And, as we have seen, those who try to separate Hero and Claudio in fact succeed in joining Beatrice and Benedick. In the most serious scene in the play – the rejection of one love – we have the establishment of another love, with the admission of Beatrice and Benedick that they are in love. The different strands of the play are thus dove-tailed together. Notice too the matching in pairs of the characters in each of the strands of the plot: Claudio with Don Pedro, Benedick with Beatrice, Dogberry with Verges, Leonato with Antonio, Borachio with Conrade, Margaret with Ursula and, though they never come together, the striking opposites of the Friar with his good advice and Don John with his evil misreportage to Don Pedro and Claudio. It will be seen from the section which follows below that the style of the play underlines the structure even to the balancing and contrasting of word-play, poetry and prose, high and low life, and imagery.

Style

Edward Dowden once wrote of Shakespeare's style that it was full of 'rapid and abrupt turnings of thought, so quick that language can hardly follow fast enough; impatient activity of intellect and fancy, which having once disclosed an idea, cannot wait to work it orderly out . . . the language is sometimes alive with imagery'. *Much Ado About Nothing* is typical of Shakespeare's middle period of activity, its poetry not being as beautiful or as poignant as that of the great tragedies but, as always, graphic and figurative language abounds.

Poetry

Vividness and variety of imagery characterize the play, but here we are concerned with it only in relation to the verse. *Much Ado* has a relatively low ratio of poetry to prose, slightly more than one quarter of it comprising the usual Shakespearian blank verse and, here, two songs. The normal line in Shakespeare's plays is a blank verse iambic pentameter, that is, a line having ten syllables. A typical example is found in Hero's:

If it prove so, then loving goes by haps;
Some Cupid kills with arrows, some with traps.

Shakespeare often uses this ten syllabled verse, here seen in a rhyming couplet to round off a sequence (Act III, I, 105-6), but in *Much Ado* the overwhelming expression is in prose, which will be examined later below. There is much variety in the verse, though, and immediately following the lines spoken by Hero above, Beatrice says:

What fire is in mine ears? Can this be true?
  Stand I condemned for pride and scorn so much?
Contempt, farewell! and maiden pride, adieu!
  No glory lives behind the back of such.

The ten-syllabled lines are here converted to a quatrain – four lines of verse with alternate lines rhyming. Generally verse is used by the noble characters in a Shakespeare play, but in *Much Ado* it is sparing because the comedy demands the freedom of quick repartee which prose can give. Thus we can pick out the poetry as characterizing those parts of the play where either elevation or potential tragedy is central to the situation. Act I moves from prose to poetry with Claudio's confiding to Don Pedro his love for Hero:

But now I am returned and that war-thoughts
Have left their places vacant, in their rooms
Come thronging soft and delicate desires . . . (281-3)

Obviously this romantic confession requires the elevation of poetry, and Don Pedro responds in like vein with his superb analogy of 'What need the bridge much broader than the flood?' (l. 296) and his determination to win Hero for Claudio, taking 'her hearing prisoner with the force/And strong encounter of my amorous tale'. The rest of the Act is in prose, since it consists of the morose Don John on the one hand, and the wit of Beatrice and Benedick on the other. But Don John's revelation to the disguised Claudio, whom he deliberately assumes to be Benedick, that Don John courts Hero for himself, causes Claudio in pathetic-tragic vein to indulge his jealousy in verse – and it is verse which reinforces the tragic element of the play:

Friendship is constant in all other things
Save in the office and affairs of love;
Therefore all hearts in love use their own tongues. (Act II, Scene 1)

When there is talk of music – and Balthasar sings – verse is naturally used to harmonize with the subject, but once the gulling of Benedick begins, prose is used as befitting the low plot. Admittedly Benedick at the end of the scene (Act II, Scene 3) has what appears to be a blank-verse line ('Fair Beatrice, I thank you for your pains') but then he too has been elevated by overhearing that he is loved.

Act III, Scene 1 has the balancing plot of Hero helped by Ursula and Margaret as prelude to the corresponding trick on Beatrice. It may at first seem strange that this is in verse, but this is probably so because the part of the women must be differentiated from that of the men, and also to display Hero to some advantage by having her talk in a more tender and less flippant fashion than her male counterparts in the previous scene. Beatrice's reaction when the other two have gone is at a more emotional level of verse which has already been quoted, her two quatrains climaxing in a scene-ending rhyming couplet.

We have already noted that Act IV Scene 1 is the climax of the play. After the preliminaries it is fittingly in verse of a rhetorical and denunciatory nature on the part of Claudio and Don Pedro; the edge of tragedy has been reached, and Claudio's words about the 'rotten orange', Don Pedro's about the 'common stale', Claudio's specific 'She knows the heat of a luxurious bed' anticipate Hamlet's fierce indictment of his own mother in his own mind. Sexual licence, or supposed sexual licence, provides Shakespeare with some of his greatest poetry, for it is the poetry of passion. Consider this in a play which is a comedy:

You seem to me as Dian in her orb,
As chaste as is the bud ere it be blown;
But you are more intemperate in your blood
Than Venus, or those pamper'd animals
That rage in savage sensuality.

We note the pagan references, always part of Shakespearian analogy, elevating the verse to a kind of universality – the references reinforcing the supposed authenticity of Claudio's injury. Leonato's own injury is reflected in verse of poignant and exclamatory power. Again the analogy with the tragedies is apparent, and, more specifically, with the tragedy of *Macbeth*. The 'multitudinous seas incarnadine' show Macbeth's blood-guilt obsession; Leonato's condemnation of his own daughter is not far removed from it:

O, she is fall'n
Into a pit of ink, that the wide sea
Hath drops too few to wash her clean again,
And salt too little which may season give
To her foul-tainted flesh!

Naturally the Friar, symbolic of goodness, utters his calming and reconciliatory thoughts in verse, since he is elevating us from sordidness and tragedy to hope of final happiness.

Some of the Friar's words are remarkable both for beauty of sentiment and expression. Consider the compression and the wisdom of the following as the Friar estimates the effect of Hero's 'death' on Claudio:

When he shall hear she died upon his words,
Th' idea of her life shall sweetly creep
Into his study of imagination
And every lovely organ of her life
Shall come apparell'd in more precious habit,
More moving-delicate and full of life,
Into the eye and prospect of his soul
Than when she liv'd indeed. (ll. 223-30)

We note here too a major Shakespearian technique in both his verse and prose, the use of repetition; the play on 'life' and 'liv'd' is a serious echo of the much lighter word-play which occurs in the other plots. In Act V Scene 1 the language of Leonato and Antonio is the language of genuine indignation and rises into poetry; as Leonato says 'Therefore give me no counsel:/My griefs cry louder than advertisement.' As long as the deception and the frustration resulting from it remains, the exchanges are in verse; with the arrival of Benedick, albeit bearing a challenge, the language is prose. Strangely, but perhaps, with method, Shakespeare has Borachio's confession to Don John and Claudio in prose but, when he is moved on Margaret's account, Borachio too speaks in verse. All the repentance speeches are in verse – of a somewhat inflated kind. Scene 3 has another departure into rhyming verse which befits the occasion of epitaph and following dirge, and this is climaxed by the final speeches of Claudio and Don Pedro, which interact with alternate lines rhyming, a clever way of indicating that they both share guilt and repentance. The last scene of the play is exclusively in verse, the high note of forgiveness, marriage and revelry being sounded by the measures and rhythms evocative of happiness.

Prose

Prose in any Shakespeare play is used with a set intent, and many instances have been recorded above in relation to Shakespeare's subtle balancing of prose and verse throughout this play. On a simplistic level, prose is the language of comic characters and characters of lower social position, Dogberry, Verges and the Watch obviously fitting both categories. These scenes representing the lower orders of society act as a contrast (note the structural coherence again) and form part of a literary convention in which aristocratic and noble characters were the chief ingredients in a play. Shakespeare is adept at showing people on a (sometimes supposedly) lower plane of feeling than that exhibited by the main characters. *Much Ado* has a majority quota of noble characters, but it is a comedy heavily dependent on wit and sharpness of repartee, which would be impossible in regular verse. Prose is therefore the natural medium for the dialogue of Beatrice and Benedick and for much of the deception plot involving what is overheard; further, Don John, Conrade and Borachio, who are not noble characters, are naturally given the same vehicle of expression. The prose of sophisticated word-play is balanced by the prose of bumbling incompetence, misplaced verbosity and misunderstanding of words which contribute to the effects of farce.

Imagery and techniques

Some examples of imagery have been given in the preceding sections. Again there is some variety. A soldier's similes and metaphors are appropriate to Benedick, who speaks of standing 'like a man at a mark, with a whole army shooting at me. She speaks poniards, and every word stabs', while he also refers disparagingly to 'these paper bullets of the brain'. This imagery serves to remind us of the war that has been fought, and of course it is part of the 'merry war' between Benedick and Beatrice. The Friar uses apt and forceful images of the time in order to illustrate Hero's innocence:

And in her eye there hath appeared a fire
To burn the errors that these princes hold
Against her maiden truth. (Act IV, Scene 1)

This is a reference to the public burning of heretics – and remember that Hero has been publicly 'burned' by Claudio's words. Hero herself, somewhat surprisingly, uses imagery which almost certainly had a topical basis when she refers to 'favourites/Made proud by princes, that advance their pride/Against the power that bred it' a comment which might apply to any number of small factions against Queen Elizabeth. Ursula, in the same conversation, uses a poetic analogy with nature:

The pleasant'st angling is to see the fish
Cut with her golden oars the silver stream,
And greedily devour the treacherous bait.

Fishing and bird analogies are used to describe the gulling of Beatrice and Benedick, but here there is a rare beauty as well as the antithesis of gold and silver. Antithesis is much used in *Much Ado,* seen in such phrases as 'Doing, in the figure of a lamb, the feats of a lion', 'A kind overflow of kindness . . . How much better is it to weep at joy than to joy at weeping.' The exchanges of Beatrice and Benedick are full of antitheses, one often completing the other's sentence by capping it with an opposite.

Satirical shafts are apparent in the play. The presentation of the Watch is satirical, though there is an almost kindly air of tolerance and forebearance in the tone. There is some satire in the presentation of Claudio and the fact that he has to have his wooing done for him, and certainly we note the satirical tone in the verbal battle between Beatrice and Benedick. Here the satire is against the force of words as distinct from the reality which lies beneath. A notable example of satire occurs when Don Pedro is speaking of Benedick in love (Act III, Scene 2); he mocks the Englishman's facility to follow the fashions of the time without discrimination, 'as to be a Dutchman today, a Frenchman tomorrow, or in the shape of two countries at once, as a German from the waist downward, all slops, and a Spaniard from the hip upward, no doublet.'

Antithesis has already been mentioned, but in *Much Ado About Nothing* Shakespeare makes much use of *euphuism,* a literary style derived from John Lyly and particularly employed in his *Euphues* (1579). It is marked not only by antithesis, often extreme, but by alliteration, extended similes, repetition and other kinds of affectation. Many or all of these are obviously present in the speech of Beatrice and Benedick. The whole of Act I Scene 3 is in this euphuistic style; a good example would be Beatrice's descanting on two words used by Benedick in thanking her for coming to fetch him in to dinner 'I took no more pains for those thanks than you take pains to thank me.' Alliteration runs throughout the play, and frequently it is accompanied by repetition. That repetition is for emphasis, but it too partakes of the word-play which is at the heart of *Much Ado About Nothing.* Here is Leonato grieving and angry at one and the same time over Hero's 'crime':

I might have said 'No part of it is mine;
This shame derives itself from unknown loins'?
But mine and mine I loved and mine I praised
And mine that I was proud on, mine so much
That I myself was to myself not mine,
Valuing of her.

In the Elizabethan period punning was extremely popular, and this often very sophisticated device of verbal trickery is second nature to most of the characters in *Much Ado About Nothing.* The double meaning is generally quite obvious, but in cases of obscurity the explanation is provided in the textual notes earlier in this commentary. Another verbal device which is used in the Dogberry scenes is that of the malapropism. It is strictly anachronistic to use the term here, since it derives from the Mrs Malaprop in Sheridan's *The Rivals* (1775), the great abuser and misuser of words. Dogberry is properly her literary and dramatic father, and his various misuses are again given in the textual notes.

Dramatic irony

This is much more commonly the effective way of heightening interest in a tragic situation, but it is used in *Much Ado*. The two most effective scenes of dramatic irony – where the audience knows something that a character or characters on stage do not know – are those involving the gulling of Beatrice and of Benedick. The audience knows they are being fooled; the characters accept what they hear and don't know they are being fooled. Perhaps the church scene is the greatest example in the play and of course the closest to the tragic use of the device. We as readers or watchers know that Hero is innocent; Leonato, Hero, Beatrice, Benedick are all ignorant of the plotting that has gone on, as indeed, in a double irony, are Claudio and Don Pedro.

Soliloquies and asides

In *Much Ado* the soliloquies are often not much more than asides, either to self or for the audience to hear. There is nothing of note until Act II Scene 1, where Claudio hears of Hero's courtship by Don Pedro from Don John, and utters an eleven-line soliloquy about false friendship and the loss of Hero. This is very effective because it gives us a foretaste of the way Claudio's mind works, his impressionability *and* his tendency to believe what he is told, seen with terrible inflexibility in church. Benedick has a superb soliloquy in Act II Scene 3 when he expatiates upon love, a soliloquy which takes on added irony in the same scene when he is gulled into believing that Beatrice loves him. Before the end of the scene, Benedick in another soliloquy convinces himself of the truth of what he has heard and vows to 'requite' Beatrice. The end of Act III Scene 1 has Beatrice alone determined to 'requite' Benedick after what she has heard.

Songs

The mood of the first song in Act II Scene 3 with its 'Sigh no more, ladies' acts as prelude to the talk of love which will lure Benedick. Both he and Beatrice are to sigh quite a bit as each realizes that the other is in love with him/her! The song in Act V Scene 3 is strictly a dirge, sung after Claudio has placed the scroll epitaph on Hero's tomb; its measures are consonant with the ritual and the formal grief expressed by the repentant Claudio.

General questions

1 Indicate the part played by chance in *Much Ado About Nothing*.

Note form suggested answer

Introduction – a paragraph on chance in the play – general.

Specific instances in paragraph 2 (a) Antonio's reporting that his man has heard Don Pedro and Claudio discussing. (b) Borachio's chance overhearing (I,3) that the Prince will woo Hero for himself and then give her to Claudio. (c) Chance that brings Beatrice and Benedick together at the masked dance, with the former not aware that Beatrice really knows who he is.

Paragraph 3 (a) The chance idea occurring to Don Pedro to gull Benedick and Beatrice. (b) The chance of the Watch stumbling upon Conrade and Borachio, and overhearing what they say. (c) Leonato's meeting with the Watch; because it is the wedding day he has by chance to go on hurriedly and therefore does not see Borachio and Conrade, whose confessions would have averted Claudio's declaration.

Paragraph 4 (a) Chance after that declaration gives the Friar the idea of the plot of Hero's 'death'. (b) This being the final 'chance' action, arguments against chance. (c) Deliberate deception (many instances throughout play) (d) Contrived plots rather than chance.

Paragraph 5 (a) Don Pedro plot re. Hero. (b) Don Pedro plot re. Benedick and Beatrice (chance or contrivance, opportunism, joke?) (c) Don John plot against Hero evolved from Borachio's idea. (d) Borachio-Margaret meeting off-stage deliberate – Claudio's and Don Pedro's presence there also arranged. (e) Sexton's presence at interrogation of Borachio/Conrade deliberate – sorts it out without chance.

Paragraph 6 Conclusion. General summing up of what is chance and what is deliberate. Own views, but weigh evidence on each side carefully.

2 Write a short essay on Shakespeare's treatment of the sources of *Much Ado About Nothing*.

3 In what ways are the main plots and the sub-plots brought into interaction in the play?

4 Write an essay on deception in *Much Ado About Nothing*.

5 In what ways is the term 'comedy' an inadequate description of the action of *Much Ado About Nothing*?

6 'Beatrice and Benedick dominate *Much Ado About Nothing*'. Discuss.

7 Write a character sketch of Claudio, saying whether you sympathize or not with his actions and reactions in the play.

8 Compare and contrast (a) Don Pedro and Leonato and (b) Don John and Borachio.

9 Write an essay on *two* of the main types of humour present in *Much Ado About Nothing*.

10 The setting of *Much Ado About Nothing* is Messina, but there is much reference to Elizabethan life and concerns. Write an account of these as they are revealed in the play.

11 Write an essay on Shakespeare's use of contrast and parallel in *Much Ado About Nothing*.

12 Indicate, by close reference to the text, the variety which Shakespeare displays in *Much Ado About Nothing*.

13 Discuss Shakespeare's use of verse and prose in *Much Ado About Nothing*.

14 Write an essay on the role and function of Dogberry in the play, bringing out by quotation the nature of the humour involved.

15 Compare and contrast (a) Hero and Margaret and (b) Dogberry and Verges.

16 Write an essay on the imagery of *Much Ado About Nothing*.

17 Write an essay on the use of punning, antithesis and any other forms of wit in the play.

18 What aspects of *Much Ado About Nothing* do you find improbable? Give reasons from the text in your answer.

19 Write a character study of any character not mentioned in the above questions.

20 Write an essay on the structure of *Much Ado About Nothing*.

Further reading

The Arden Shakespeare: Much Ado About Nothing, ed. A. R. Humphreys (Methuen 1981). Read particularly the Introduction.

The Signet Shakespeare: Much Ado About Nothing, ed. D. L. Stevenson (New American Library, 1964).

Political and Comic Characters of Shakespeare, John Palmer (Macmillan 1946, reissued 1961).

Shakespeare's Happy Comedies, John Dover Wilson (Faber 1962).

Shakespeare's Comedies: An Anthology of Modern Criticism, ed. Laurence Lerner (Penguin Shakespeare 1967).

Much Ado About Nothing, J. R. Mulryne (Edward Arnold 1965).

Shakespeare's Comedies, Ralph Berry (Princeton U.P. 1972).